Northern T

ISBN: 978-0-9565018-0-6

Poetry and Prose
by
Northern Co-operative Writers and friends

Published on behalf of
Northern Co-operative Writers by:

Carillon Magazine
19 Godric Drive,
Brinsworth, Rotherham,
South Yorkshire. S60 5AN

e-mail: *editor@carillonmag.org.uk*
web site: *http://www.carillonmag.org.uk*

All enquiries and orders
should be sent to the above address

First published February 2010
reprinted July 2010

04646993

This book is a co-operative production by writers in Yorkshire and adjacent areas

Published by

Carillon Magazine

http://www.carillonmag.org.uk

for

Northern Co-operative Writers

http://www.ncwriteon.org.uk

Cover © by Julia Pearson

Printed in the UK by:
Inky Little Fingers Ltd
Unit A3, Churcham Business Park
Churcham,
Gloucester, GL2 8AX

www.inkylittlefingers.co.uk

Foreword

Ninety-eight texts from fifty-one writers in over twenty locations; contributors ranging from well-respected published authors and editors to some new writers, providing content and styles ranging from the very traditional to the very modern: as an eclectic a mix as we could possibly have hoped for when the project was first mooted several months ago.

So, first, we want to thank every contributor: you have helped provide an interesting and entertaining collection and we hope that you feel the book has done you justice.

Thanks, too, for those who spread the word and encouraged others to participate. There are many names new to us within these pages and we've been particularly delighted by the tremendous support from the York area.

Northern Co-operative Writers sprang out of a discussion during a Rotherham meeting around the end of 2008. Chris Bilton took up the challenge and, early in 2009, launched an online Forum on ning.com which was developing very nicely until it was hit by a massive, ongoing and unstoppable spam attack, forcing us to close it down. A new Forum should be opened before long: watch our web site for the new link.

This publication is NCW's first major project. What next? We're not sure yet, but we hope one day to actually meet people (Ideas very welcome). Of course, being self-funded, we are very much limited by financial considerations.

We hope you enjoy reading this book , and if you can sell a few copies for us, we'd be grateful. Any profits made will be ploughed back into the NCW Forum.

Wishing you a fruitful and rewarding 2010,

Graham Rippon

Contributors

Peter Asher	Scunthorpe
Chris Bilton	Rotherham
Roy Blackman	Rotherham
Brian Blackwell	Leeds
Terry Boyle	Rotherham
Della Brighton	Doncaster
Zoe Broome	Lincoln
Helen Burke	York
F. Mary Callan	York
Shilpi Chakraborty	Sheffield
David Cooke	Grimsby
John Critchley	Doncaster
Simon Freeman	Sheffield
Linda Gamston	Rotherham
Simon Gore	Sheffield
Barbara Gummerson	Grimethorpe
Oz Hardwick	York
Ray Hearne	Rotherham
Ann Heath	York
Alan Hurst	Rotherham
Peter Johnson	Burley-in-Wharfedale
Pauline Kirk	York
Patrick Lodge	York
Ian Lowery	Huddersfield
Steve Mawson	Rotherham

Contributors

Julie Mellor	Penistone
Susan Mary Morgan	Barugh Green
Andy McMaster	Retford
Daithidh MacEochaidh	Hebden Bridge
Steven Nash	York
Marion New	Oxspring
Keith Newing	Rotherham
David Norris-Kay	Sheffield
Muriel Noton	Sheffield
Julia Pearson	Silkstone
Graham Rippon	Rotherham
Barbara Robinson	Boston Spa
Miles Salter	York
Kerry Louise Sheridan	Sheffield
Vic Speight	Barnsley
Adrian Spendlow	York
John Stocks	Sheffield
Paul Sutherland	Market Rasen
Jemma Sykes	Rotherham
Adrian Tellwright	York
Christine May Turner	Rotherham
Clint Wastling	York
A. K. Whitehead	Pontefract
Bernadette Whiteley	Darton
Sue Whittaker	York
Louise Wilford	Elsecar

Peter Asher (Scunthorpe)

Twitch

The brief case contained
when it was stolen -
A poem and some stories -
all of them golden

Any one line could
have bettered man's lot -
But the thief was concerned
with the case that he got

And the poem and the stories
were thrown to the ground
Like an old lady's purse
when the money's been found

By the thief - and the poem
and the stories were cast
To the side and just left
upon the wet grass

And lost to the world
which remained impoverished
For that absence of wisdom
rotting in the twitch

But it wasn't the wisdom
the old lady missed
So much as the money
from the purse in that ditch.

Chris Bilton   (Rotherham)

The Descent

He climbs, as does the Dark Peak
looking down with grizzled gaze
through snow thrown frost,
man dangles miles over nothing.

Fangs of granite chiselled with ice
blaze across his empty face as
hands twitch for anchorage
To no avail, footing finds fresh air.

He loses grip, the sky is then earth
the ground becomes the sky now
weightless with a ton of gear
rope reels from his rag-doll form.

He hears deep inside the Peak
a jagged sigh then a roar from
a demon throat awake with ore
his thoughts tremble, then quiet.

Through the silver sting of eyes
man scratches trough tint of hue
that fleck the chill as marking path
towards a golden fissure yawning.

Shards of light cut his chilled spirit
stepping between cascading souls
essence is torn free from his flesh
as a warm hand reaches his cold heart.

The Street

Mock flock
Wallpaper in
pebbledash pink.
Babies bottle
tarmaced into road
with a spit pool
Neatly to the left.
Through window
a Spanish lady
shelf dances.
Dinner smells.
A sea gull fly
past green
non-recyclable
wheelie bin.

2

Chris Bilton   (Rotherham)

War Zone

Flaming sky's quiver with the hymn of casualties
in the bitter sun's heat. No traceable season,
the sclerosis oil pool bristles as the bombs grin
and strike down through black hooded clouds.
Soulless eyes tune to this warmonger hermit wind,
it cuts out the tongue of all that dare to speak.
They were companions to a dark world,
no welcome for the hearts of careless men.
Jawbones lock to the skull; talk will have to wait
guns crank with muscular life and the
victim's skull gives a silent yawn.
By blood bound a soul without spring is lost.

We Buried Him Under The Patio

Two summers ago, sitting around,
the evening's rhythm was quickly set
with drink and conversation.

The thing about real illness is
it lets your conscience off the hook,
she said, with insight too close for comfort.

Clouds swung in like an iron gate as the
smell of rain on its way flicked at the awning
bar coding shadows on the patio floor.

That unrealness that comes with remembering
a close one passing gave the senses a fillip,
not unpleasant if taken on a sunny day.

Well he passed away in bed so that's okay, I said,
my voice dropping as though taken out by
a snipers bullet, hopefully snuffing any emotion.

He's still with us, she said, yes said I,
gripping my inner sandal soles with my toes
and slapping the patio floor.

Roy Blackman   (Rotherham)

Autumn Leeds

It's autumn, when hanging baskets droop like willows.
On Holbeck Weir the Aire roars thin 'neath scudding clouds
And City Market air raws thin with strawberries down.
Marge has packed in Dave she met on Kos.
High on Benzene mixed with mist, Baz and Bradford speedway
Morcambe illuminations beckon charas in hordes via Skipton.
By the Corn Exchange's gloom the gleaming bus lights roll.

It's autumn, the rain spits in and out of Briggate,
Where Mr Bernstein unrolls his Christmas decorations.
Delroy stirs his last burger's onions in Potter Newton Park
And sniffs the mustard where the rhododendrons rust.
At Otley Folkfest, Ray Hearne sings of Thurnscoe
While Jimmy Saville wheezes to his old age pension
And *Look North* covers all the party conferences.
It's autumn, when Monet colours in the Liverpool Express
Rallentando to a Hunslet Turner sunset - grumbling, rumbling
Under Thunder Bridge's blackberry banks, past an unexpected wood.
Kids collect conkers, a squirrel waits his chance
For food by a chestnut brook; swifts flock gold shines on another bridge.
Meanwhile Darren Gough, eyes turned up skywards, pauses, prepares,
One last bouncer before autumn leaves Leeds

Roy Blackman   *(Rotherham)*

Dettol

Aunt Jill was perpetual motion and Dettol.
The house reeked of it
Like the paediatric ward where she worked.
Her ham sandwiches tasted of it.
You asked for a second cup of tea
If you didn't mind the burning taste.
She listened to Mrs Dale's Diary;
All the time the sounds of scouring - *Cleanliness is next to Godliness.*
Aunt Jill wore blue, sang *Rule Britannia*
As she worked.
She terrified the doctors, the vicar,
And the local Lord of the Manor. Her caustic aggression ruled.
Our village had the best child health care figures in Britain.
The MP ran when he saw her coming.
The local beggar gave HER 20p
And she accepted it.
On the day she died
The Peace Memorial collapsed.

(Roy is very well known in South Yorkshire and beyond as a poet and performance poet of note. His "Folk Opera" based on the miners strike has been performed at various venues around the region. The two poems here are taken from his book, "Roy's Ruskin Collection")

Brian Blackwell   (Leeds)

Mother

I kissed your warm cheek.
I noticed your blooded lips.
I was aware of a stained, soaked sheet
beneath your motionless form.

Eyes closed
you'd see no more;
you'd think no more;
you'd feel no more.

There's nothing to remember now
and nothing to forget. You are free.

There's a bursting out of silence
and stillness, like the opening
of a hard-shaken magnum of champagne:
but a silent bang.

The bang of absolute awareness,
of absolute love.
A silent awareness,
a deafening love:
acute, pained, unending,
even pervading relief
like a dedication.

Open as a cracked dam,
wet as cascading tears.

Brian Blackwell   (Leeds)

"A stillness of waiting"   (Henry Moore)

Silences like stillnesses
are at one with emptiness
and fullness, knowing how to cope
with doubt and resting on the richness
of fulfilment, transcending

the vogue of tradition, unshackling
from habit and convention,
building rapport with elemental
metaphor. The curve of an embryo
hurtling through time and space.

A succulent fruit, its future
about to burst, to explore new worlds;
the line of a sensual breast to caress,
sheer love, to feed new young and amplify
the dignity of ultimate worth.

This grandeur, this monumental joy
transcends the emptiness and fullness
of mere stillnesses and silences, it welds
their emotion, their energy, to bond
dynamic minds. The waiting has gained

a stillness. Gained the reverence of silence,
has grown from awareness and pain,
from the fusion of the infinite and finite,
the real and the unreal, the truth in the stone,
a stillness of waiting.

Terry Boyle   (Rotherham)

It's Not So Easy

It's not so easy watching
As your loved one's mind goes,
Slowly but then quickly
Like frost ravaging a rose.
Though she changes daily,
Still you care with every breath
But deep inside you cry
And curse this living death.

So you try to make her happy,
Try to make her life complete,
You become her memory
And make sure that she eats.
You even buy her food
Though you do not drip with wealth,
And deep inside you're screaming
About her mental health.

You see her every weekday
But always keep back one
Just to give yourself some time
And maybe have some fun.
But you think about her constantly
And worry that she's fine
And deep inside you rage
That you're a selfish swine.

Then comes the day you see her
And she's erudite and well:
A little bit of heaven
Pokes through this living hell.
You see the real person
And remember why you care,
But deep inside you know
That soon she won't be there.

Terry Boyle   (Rotherham)

N.I.M.B.Y.

In Mexborough live the ignorant:
They're frightened and insecure,
Afraid that mental illness
Is knocking on the door.

They think it is unfair,
This terror they cannot see:
(I quote)
"I know they must be somewhere
But don't put them close to me."

They've found a legal loophole
To close down Aspen House
While tolling humanity's death knell
As with venom they douse

The dreams and aspirations
Of the people living there
Rejected by community
Who, frankly, couldn't care.

Safe in their terraced houses
Where they're all feeling fine,
Unaware that one in four of them
Could become ill at any time.

Rotherham Metro Writers

Meets every 2nd Tuesday of the month
at the Trades Club,
Greasbrough Road, Rotherham
at 7.40 pm
Leader: Terry Boyle

Enquiries to the Secretary, Graham Rippon,
at the "Carillon" address on the Title Page of this book.
e-mail to: grippon1@tiscali.co.uk

Della Brighton   (Doncaster)

Down With the Clown

Clown, your feet are massive
And your wig is way too big
Your make-up's like the front man
At a Heavy Metal gig.

And Clown, your great big eyebrows -
They are like Alsatian fur
And who is it decides upon
Those awful clothes you wear.

Now, Clown, don't think I'm rotten,
But your jokes are not that good.
That's why the crowd were pelting you
With chunks of Yorkshire pud.

Hey, Clown, maybe it's time for you
To call time on the clown
And pack away your tired act
And pompom hat and gown.

All Bunged Up

Stuffy nose, throat is sore
Barking louder, stay indoors
Hardly hungry, cheeks aglow
Need for speed, but moving slow

Rasping voice, head is grumpy
Fever high and throat is lumpy
Patience now, must take my time
Another week, I'll feel just fine.

Della Brighton   (Doncaster)

A Year Through The Seasons

January winter berries
February sneezes
March brings Spring so let's be merry
April sends the breezes
May you may not need a coat
June flowers all around
July hills full of lambs and goats
August bakes the ground
Come September blooms fade
October trees look stunning
November leaf tints now degrade
December, yuletide's coming.

Zoe Broome   (Lincoln)

First Friend

My first friend,
we played alone on the playground.

We fitted each role:
Cop, Batman, son -
Robber, Robin, mother.

My first friend,
we laid our coats on the grass to play friendly football.
I scored 90 goals against the school goalie.

We played each game together:
you taught me to win, then I beat you.
Somewhere, grownups reversed fortunes.

My first friend,
we longed to be bikers, heroes or footballers.

We stole apples from teacher
when she wasn't looking.

My first friend
before you left, you learned to spit.
I told you not to.
You said some things are worth spitting at.

Should we meet now,
I wouldn't recognise you.
You wouldn't notice me,
your first friend.

Zoe Broome   (Lincoln)

Cemetery: Early Morning

I wake early. Deciding to invest
the rest of night in silence, mark the dead.
Their brittle bodies wrapped in winter rest,
Covered in mud. Ghosts made me leave my bed.

Branches are bare above the melting snow.
The graveyard's full. Each tomb's replete with bones.
I feel that there's something I don't yet know.
And as I pass, I mark each saint, each stone.

I step into a tomb: a rocky grave.
Somebody's died. Sharp sadness should be here.
But sunlight breaks through the cracks of this grave -
A young man's come in. He laughs, lacks fear.

In death's coldness I saw the early dawn,
A laughing child. Magic stood out from scorn.

Fire of New Year

The beach is flickering firelight
welcoming New Year into the coast.
It's a lighthouse: letting the year inland.

A dog barks a warning, remember the last -
December is only a day ago.
I don't listen. Fire burns the old year.

Cliffs crumble, shops open, a world changes
without a plan like a day tripper it stumbles in.
Now the beach is flickering firelight.

Helen Burke   (York)

On Meeting Dracula at the Blood Transfusion Wagon

There's just something about him, we know it from the first.
But – the rest of them - seem blind.
The women buzz around his black coat-tails.
He moves effortlessly, his eyes
dark as double pansies.
When the shadow from them catches you –
as if the heart is sudden-stung.
"What a sweetie," one girl says.
"So pale and wild and interesting."
He swoops on her hand, kisses it.
She stands frozen, cannot bat an eyelid.
Even the old ladies plump up their almost curls and
try to look wrinkle-free for Mr. D.
"Cup of tea?" one offers him.
"No thanks," he says –
"I've had so much to drink today, I'm
positively swimming, don't you know."
It's alarming how charming he is.
The little pointy teeth clatter in his mouth
as he sucks a mint imperial.
In a certain light, he seems harmless – and yet...
The brass catch at his throat in the shape of a rabid wolf –
how fearsome delicate.
The glint of a red-eyed bat at the top of his glossy walking cane.
It's almost too much to bear.
I look away as a girl offers him a chip.
I can hear the soft squelch of the ketchup bottle as he licks his salty lips.
"You'll go far, my dear," he whispers in the pale ivory conch of her ear.
We wander into town to clear our heads (have to).
But later, when we pass the red and white van –
we see it is CLOSED but the lights are still on.
Inside – a woman who thought she could tame him
about to find out – it has all been in vain.

Helen Burke   (York)

The Green Field

I dreamed I was a horse
and the green field all around me
kissed my feet.
In my eyes two doves smiled
and the sun and moon were mine
in equal measure.
The day was music within my bones.
The night was music within my blood
and I was blessed.

And blessed
I ran within that green field, where,
in its sweetest, farthest corner I saw
lay buried, a silver-box – so small,
yet within the box,
lay the root, the tree,
the waiting forest of my dreams.

And from this, - I ran.
And ran, and ran, far, far from it, until –
at last, I saw it no more –
and was sad.
For years I ran and ran and ran – until –
the moon it was that stopped me. Under her light,
I looked down and saw that
within my own body lay that green field,
within my own heart lay that silver box.
Still and silent   in the moon's light.

Waiting.

*(Helen is a York poet/visual artist
who does a lot of national and local readings
see web site www.poetrypf.co.uk)*

15

F. Mary Callan (York)

In The Dayroom

"Put your own teeth in!" snapped Little Red Riding Hood.

The Wolf stared mournfully at the dish of pulverised swede she had plonked on his invalid table. He wouldn't need his teeth after all. Drat television! And drat documentaries that proved the dog family could support life on a vegetarian diet! He picked up the remote control and chomped it gummily, just to teach it a lesson.

Little Red Riding Hood slammed her trolley into the dispense area and stamped into the tea kitchen. Another government report! another Heptagon* initiative to promote animal amity and desegregation between species! As if her feet weren't killing her! As if she wasn't breaking no-minister-knew-how-many regulations by losing her tea break and snatching this non-regulation cuppa in the residents' kitchen!

It was only a grant from the Ministry of Culture which had provided sties for the Three Little Pigs, now more accurately referred to as the Three Large Pigs, or politely as the Three Horizontally -Enhanced Porkines, since horizontal was all they ever were these days. Seventeen weeks' paperwork had been needed to get that grant! and only after a supporting statement from the Ministry of Fur and Feathers expressing deep concern that the number of broken legs sustained by ostriches falling over the recumbent Three Horizontally-Enhanced Porkines was a national scandal, and would threaten the future of the whole Animal Heroes Retirement venture. She slumped in her chair, and laid her head on the table.

Granny automatically crocheted another round, before noticing what had woken her up. That wasn't NEIGHBOURS (in which, thanks to Heptagon initiatives, Skippy the kangaroo's grand-children and a family of possums now had leading roles). The Wolf''s grumbling had had unpredictable results, and the present broadcast showed a cheery young chef suggesting practical recipes for the planned colonies on Mars. His studio partner was a colourful snake, and, despite Heptagon directives, the young man was treating it with more respect than trust.

Using her stick to launch her chair into a wheelie, Granny spun across to the Wolf, and thumped his back to change channels; then quickly out of reach before he could complain.

Thursdays were a bit pointless: with the Three Horizontally-Enhanced Porkines' mother at her yoga class, there was no other granny in the dayroom to show off to.

16

The Wolf merely nodded if she boasted about Red Riding Hood and her achievements as matron. He nodded whatever you said these days. Would her vague plan to tuck this crocheted blanket round him when it was finished, kindle the last of his fury, and let them feel some of the danger that had once made life interesting? If not, Heptagon initiatives were the only hope.

She dozed again, imagining how it might happen when the Three Horizontally-Enhanced Porkines, and the ostriches, took up residence in the ward: the Wolf, with his 'last reserves of strength!' lunging out of his chair and breaking his grey neck on the parquet. Would they have to cremate him, or would the Department of Ethnic Artefacts allow them to keep him as a rug?

Successor to the Pentagon, with two extra angles.

Visit Mary's web site : http://www.notsodeadpoet.com

Shilpi Chakraborty   (Sheffield)

My Husband's Old Flame

I am not a Bollywood movie buff. If I were asked to say a few words on this genre by swearing on the Bible, I would have pretty nasty things to say about the recent lowbrow kitsch our moviemakers were dishing out. But let me keep those thoughts to myself, the last thing I would want is to sound smug. Just a few days back my husband told me that he would like to watch the Bollywood movie *Rock on* with me. I had seen the promos on television and kind of liked it. It looked urbane, chic, contemporary, and a throwback to the days of *Dil Chahta hai* (another Bollywood movie about three friends their lives and their ideals). We watch movies on our laptop. Theatre halls had become out of bounds for us since our son was born. Now, he is three-and-a half, yet we don't have the confidence or the cheek to go to a movie hall. I don't have the stamina to scurry after him in the dark alleys, answer his onslaught of questions, nor can I be blasé about the frowns on the faces of harried audience. Though watching movie in a laptop is not a great cinematic experience, we have become used to it by now. Few minutes into the movie, and I could see a faraway look in my husband's eyes. He was already in the arms of nostalgia. I squeezed his hands, he understood what I meant. It was okay to feel nostalgic. Reel life and real life can sometimes be as different as chalk and cheese and sometimes they are so similar that they seem to overlap each other.

Like Aditya, the protagonist in the movie, my husband too was a member of a music band. He and three of his friends had formed it in their heady Engineering College days. Well, it is blasphemous to talk about it in past tense. It very much exists. Anyway, they were fired by the zeal to make good music. The band was the labour of their love. They penned lyrics, wrote music and also gave the vocals. And their music did strike a chord. It was lapped up by the college crowd. They were in hog's heaven when they heard sounds of their music floating out of hostel rooms and friends crooning and humming their numbers. Like all cub musicians, they too wanted to set the stage afire, belt out numbers, make the crowd delirious and cut an album.

After college, MNC's beckoned. With plum jobs came the banes attached to it, nerve-grating work pressure, cut-throat competition and long working hours, and their dream got caught in the corporate maelstrom. It would be wrong to say they folded their dreams like woollens and nudged it into a corner of the cupboard with the onset of summer. They did give it a shot. They participated in a few talent-hunt shows, visited music studios and met a few music stalwarts in India to further their cause. But, every time, their efforts went pear shaped. By then the fire of their passion had fizzled out somewhat. Priorities changed. They were no longer youths without a care in the world but responsible family men. With time they drifted away. But unlike the film, there was no bad blood nor did they shut each other out of their lives. They are still very much in touch and good buddies. It is a different fact that they now live in three different countries. My husband is still very passionate about music.

A few days after our arrival in UK, he went to a musical instrument shop and bought himself a guitar. "Can't live without it," he told me, pointing to his old flame. He still strums the guitar, pens lyrics and composes music, but now it takes him many moons to complete a song. Can't blame him. Whenever he takes out his guitar from its case, my mercurial son is all over him. He yanks it away from him and runs his Thomas and friends trains on the strings. "This is my track," he says. His college friends, now a click away, thanks to social networking websites, tell him how they still listen to their songs. Some bemoan their inability to put their creations on the music landscape, while some are always ready with a litany of advice.

In the film, the friends reunite, live their dream once more and move on. My husband got all misty-eyed after the movie. I realized life rarely works out the way we want it to; many a time, dreams get swept under the carpet and we hardly recognize the face staring back at us out of the mirror. I held his hand and sat quiet for some time. Our son was scribbling away on his aqua-draw mat with a water-filled pen.

A few seconds later the scribbles started to fade away. My husband wriggled free out of my grip and said, "I can't let my dreams vanish into thin air like these scribbles. I think I gave up on my dream pretty soon. Also, it would be wrong to believe that one day my son will live my dream. His dreams might be very different from mine."

He walked off and sat in front of his computer. I watched as he frantically tapped away on the keyboard. I knew he was emailing his band members.

They replied. My husband was not satisfied with their response, so he decided to march ahead alone. As of now, he has decided to start a web site with their songs, and is also planning to add new songs to their collection. His creative juices are flowing again. He composed a new song, dedicated to my son, downloaded recording software from the Net, recorded it in his own voice and uploaded it on You Tube. And he got pretty good reviews.

I don't know whether he will realize his dream, but I am happy to see that he is still ploughing on. True stories inspire cinema and again it is vice versa.

David Cooke   (Grimsby)

Shadow Boxing

The closest my dad ever got to poetry
was when he savoured some word
like *pugilist,* or the tip-toe springiness
he sensed in *bob and weave,*
his unalloyed delight in the flytings
and eyeball to eyeball hype
that went with big fight weigh-ins.

And perhaps I too might have been
a contender when I did my stint
in the ring, my dad convinced
I had the style and stamp of a winner,
when in the end I just got bored.
You had to have a killer's instinct,
to do much better than a draw.

In the gym the lights are low.
It's after hours. I'm on my own.
The boards are rank with sweat
and stale endeavour. Shadow boxing
like the best of them, I will show
him feints, a classic stance,
trying always to keep up my guard.

David Cooke   (Grimsby)

Grammar School

It had all started so well with a brand new
leather briefcase, its status enhanced
by its clasp and key, and its concertina sections
for work we now called *subjects.*

The first time I opened it up
I got the whiff of weighty matters –
a prize that was only eclipsed
by the drop-handled racer

they bought to get me there –
though that was to prove almost fatal
when a juggernaut caught me on its blind side
as we pulled off at the lights.

Two months later and my bones
were fixed, while the bike barely survived –
a few parts salvaged, then grafted on
to a botched-up frame

that was hand-painted, hulking.
Up Berkley Avenue's slow incline
it sapped my strength
like a lifetime's disappointment.

John Critchley   (Doncaster)

A Saturday Afternoon Out

I couldn't see any trains going to Hull on the VDU.

"You do know there are no direct trains to Goole?" asked the concerned-looking young woman sat behind the protective screen in the ticket office at Doncaster Railway Station. I didn't, but did have a plan B to fall back on. I was going to have a Saturday afternoon out somewhere, I seldom don't in the football season.

"Make that Guiseley instead," my reply, though I usually get a South Yorkshire Day-Tripper on the bus and a Day-Return from South Elmsall - about five pounds cheaper that way. The Express service to Leeds on time and just about sufficient of it to get a quick pint of real ale before joining the train for Ilkley. The Station always my first port of call there after phoning home. Tetley's and Sky Sports. No time for another, just enough for a Copper Dragon and a Jack Daniels and ice before kick-off.

Guiseley versus Kings Lynn. Six of the away side over six feet tall including three giant central defenders that the home side could not figure a way through, round or over until they were already beaten. Same again at the bar at half-time and in The Station and I'm onboard the Leeds train at seventeen twenty hours phoning home that I'm on my way.

The London train standing at platform eight, two minutes before take off, but crammed full, Leeds United at home. Solution: retire to the Weatherspoon's for a pint of cider and to watch England on the telly and wait for the next one. Wayne Rooney getting a penalty and Frank Lampard dispatching it.

I find a seat, not always easy. One minute to go and I'm glad I had the Cornish Pasty and mushy peas at the ground. Then an announcement that someone had been killed at Wakefield Westgate Railway Station and everyone had to detrain; those travelling south of *Wakey* had to do so via York.

The York service ten minutes late and very few people from the London train waiting on the platform and another phone home to explain the situation. The London service standing in on platform three at Yorkshire's capital city, only it isn't by the time I roll up. Still, only half an hour to the next one and there always Coopers outside, three pounds fifteen pence for a pint of cider in a plastic glass and three hen parties in full swing, I giving up my seat so one of the three could all sit together - they saying I was a gentleman - I do try.

One of the hen parties dressed as a policewoman talking to a gang of football fans that had been to see their team play at York City, I didn't bother asking who they supported or cared by then, but they had southern accents and the look of a soccer hooligan crew, one of them constantly on the mobile. No doubt they had a spotter out somewhere - I've read the books, seen the films and the famous Blades' Business Crew in action over the years. My train due, or so I thought. Delayed by half an hour. Another over-priced Strongbow in a plastic glass stood up after another call home. All the seats taken by then and the southerners nowhere to be seen.

I am on the move, finally. Doncaster here I come at last. Two Green Un's purchased in the newsagents in Donny Bus Station, I always get one for my dad who only ever watches Sheffield United at Bramall Lane now, no non-league excursions for him, and read mine on the Sunday when I'm sober.

The Edlington bus to Balby, fish and chips, no mushy peas I had them in West Yorkshire and home by nine o'clock to tell the tale. Strangely, I've never seen Harry Ramsden's or a sign for it at Guiseley - it's birthplace.

There nothing on the news or Ceefax about any murder at Wakefield or why there were no direct trains to Goole, probably engineering work at Thorne, there's none to Scunthorpe or Cleethorpes either. Replaced by coaches, only I don't do those if at all possible, take too long in my experience and never arrive where or when you expect them too.

Hallam Football Club next week, bus, train and Supertram and home by nineteen hundred hours at the latest, fingers crossed.

Simon Freeman   (Sheffield)

Mama's Little Soldier

"I hate you!"

"No you don't. You don't know the meaning of the word."

Daniel sulked. Now Mum was ignoring him. If he'd been twenty years older and read the 'Guide to Good Parenting' he'd have realised she was using a tactic of ignoring bad behaviour so he didn't feel he was getting attention by throwing tantrums. He had wanted some chocolate though. Why did Mum always say it would just spoil his tea? That or we can't afford it today. Funny how they could always afford her glass of wine or Dad's beer.

"If you're going upstairs take your shoes off. Why don't you stay outside until tea's ready? It's a lovely day."

"Want a pen and paper."

"I've a writing pad in the drawer over there Why don't you write Gran a nice letter thanking her for your birthday present."

He took the writing implements outside and down to the den he and Dad had made at the bottom of the garden, two benches with bricks for legs and planks for seats and an old coffee table Auntie Vi had chucked out.

"Dear Mum and Dad," he wrote."I've runaway to join the army." He weighted the note down with a stone and left it on the table before picking up his red scooter and wheeling it to the gate of the semi-detached house. He opened it carefully. It tended to squeak as Dad hadn't oiled it. Then it was quickly away, his left foot on the scooter board and his right pushing him along for all it was worth, along Painter Road, round the corner and up Hallow Brook Avenue and past the junction with Hallow Brook Lane to the shops.

What now? You couldn't join the army at Mr. Graham's hardware shop or the Co-op although the latter did sell chocolate. Daniel couldn't go in there though. The till lady, Pat, talked to his Mum and she'd tell on him. What was this though? The shop between them which had been empty for weeks was showing signs of life and it looked very much like a sweet shop.

Daniel laid his scooter down in the doorway. Inside was a man. He turned and beckoned Daniel inside. His Mum said you shouldn't talk to strangers and he was scared but this man was wearing a uniform and that meant in Daniel's eyes that you could trust him. He pushed the glass door open.

Hullo,"said the man."What do you want."

I want some chocolate and I want to join the army."

"Well you've come to the right place. I've got a chocolate army in here."

On the shelves stood rows and rows of chocolate soldiers wrapped in tin foil with scarlet uniforms and busby hats. Daniel looked at the shopkeeper. His uniform was brown, his sergeants' stripes were brown and his face and eyes and teeth were brown. He handed Daniel a bar of chocolate.

"That's your first day's wages, and if you sign this form here you'll be all signed up. I see you've got a pen."

Daniel took the paper from the recruiting sergeant and the pen he'd brought from home from his shirt pocket. He read the form. It was written in grown-up words he didn't understand, but there was a bit in the middle about signing up for ten years and not being allowed home for holidays, even birthdays and Christmas. He looked at the faces of the chocolate soldiers. They didn't look like soldiers at all, but like little boys and girls.

The recruiting sergeant was on the phone now, an old fashioned black Bakelite one with a thick black cable linking it to the receiver. "I've just bagged another one sir!"

Daniel looked at the pen. It was one he and Mum had chosen and given to Dad as a Fathers Day present. He fought the urge to cry. He wasn't going to join up. Instead he dropped the paper and fled for the door.

"Hey, come back," shouted the sergeant ."I've given you your wages. I'll clap you in irons."

Daniel had got through the door and was reaching for his scooter when he felt the hand touch his shoulder. Instinctively he turned and thrust the pen he was still holding into the man's eye.

The sergeant screamed. "You bad boy! I'll have you shot!"

Daniel leapt on his scooter as the sergeant staggered after him. It was hot and the sun was shining and as he sped away Daniel looked back and saw the man starting to melt. Within minutes Daniel was home. He flung his scooter down in the back yard and went into the kitchen. No Mum. Then he heard her voice. Had she missed him and reported it to the police or rung Dad at work to come home and look for him?

Next day they went for walk to the park. On the way back they called at the Co- op and bought some bread. Mum talked to Pat for hours about some woman on TV whose clothes they didn't like before they went to Mr Graham to buy some lightbulbs. The shop between the two was empty, no chocolate soldiers, and no recruiting sergeant.

"I heard someone was going to take it but changed their mind," said Mum.

Daniel felt a shiver run down his spine. He looked down at the floor and saw something glisten. It was Dad's birthday pen, covered in sticky chocolate. He looked up. Mum was distracted, looking at something in Mr Graham's shop window. She always told him not to pick things up in the street, but she couldn't see and he thought he'd make an exception for this. With a bit of luck he'd sneak it back in the drawer and they'd never realise it had been missing.

Sheffield Writers Club

Sheffield Writers Club has been on the go for some 40 or 50 years which makes it the longest running organisation of the kind in our area.

Meetings are held fortnightly
at the Quaker Meeting House
(near the Cathedral Tram Stop)
5.00 PM
on alternate Wednesdays.

Members pay a contribution of £2.00 per meeting to pay for the cost of room and refreshments.

Contact John Nettleship
Sheffield (0114) 2668641

Details of future meetings are posted on the Writers Information Board in Sheffield Central Library.

Linda Gamston   *(Rotherham)*

The Yorkshire Range

Much more than an oven wer' t'old Yorkshire range,
and some folk might even think it wer' strange
that you could not only cook, but warm t' feet for a change.

Bread and rice puddings cooked in it wer' t' best,
and lemon curd turned out better than t' rest,
and you could warm up some oil to rub on your chest.

Twice a week lots o' dough wer' on t' hearth to rise,
to make loaves for six (ten in t' war) – a good size,
and ma wer' so proud when she won a bakin' prize.

Ma black leaded t' range every weekend,
then cooked Sunday dinner, so as to tend
to all o' t' family and sometimes a friend.

Tasty, crisp onions cooked slowly by t' fire,
and t' kettle boiled on it or on t' bar that wer' higher,
but some mishaps were a little more dire.

Granddad put shoe polish in t' oven to melt,
and it spat all o'er t' room, and grandmother felt
angry, and chased him around wi' his belt.

Dad sat there wi' his toes up, to toast 'em,
but snoozed, and didn't realise he'd roast 'em!
He hobbled for days, wi' a face like a ghost, then.

We all got up early to chop wood in a rush
to make t' fire, and cleaned t' flue wi' a brush
so t' soot wouldn't come down in a big mucky gush.

T' baby had pneumonia, and wer' wrapped in cotton wool
and put in t' oven wi' her belly nice and full,
to keep warm and get better, wi' a soft song to lull.

A tin bath in front made us clean, warm and red,
we had t' oven shelves and hot bricks for cold feet in bed,
and wi' that old range we were all right well fed.

My favourite wer' toast done on a long fork
in front o' t' embers – it wer' as good as pork.
and that Yorkshire range wer' worth all t' mucky work.

Simon Gore   (Sheffield)

Words

I have words
I want to write
But they'll never
See the light

My pen and I
Used to be friends
But all he's writing
Is dead ends

I put him down
Use another
But they talk
Collude together

It's not fair
They won't obey me
But i'll get them one day
Just wait and see

I think I've beat them
My words now flow
But what am I writing
No, NO, NO

Obey me damn you
I'm your master
I start to scribble
Faster and faster

I read it back
And then I die
All my words
Are a lie

They confess to things
That I've not done
My mind recalls
The terrible fun

So there you have it
My pen likes to say
Me and my friend
Locked away!

Simon Gore   (Sheffield)

Hands

I like my Hands, they're always there, at the end of my arms.

Mum always used to say, "Keep your Hands clean and your fingers out of other peoples business".

Well I wished I'd listened, you see my Hands have done some really dirty, nasty evil things. I've heard the count is now 14, but that can't be true can it?

Wish I'd listened to my Mum!

Barbara Gummerson (Grimethorpe, Barnsley)

I Will Go...

I will go gentle into that good night
Having danced with time and dined with devotion.
I will not rage at the dying of the light.

This life, without regret, has touched delight,
And laughed and cried, and loved with deep emotion.
I will go gentle into that good night.

And life with all its limbo cannot blight
Content. I've sailed the crest of life's ocean.
I will not rage at the dying of the light.

Let life never lose touch with what is right,
Or being wrong, without the least commotion
I will go gentle into that good night.

With life's large journey to endure, take flight,
Contribute love and peace, despite corrosion.
I will not rage at the dying of the light.

Sweet life, gain and do forgive or be slight,
With truth, in tact and tender motion.
I will go gentle into that good night.
I will not rage at the dying of the light.

Barbara Gummerson   (Grimethorpe, Barnsley)

Aware

The more I look, the more I love this life: this
wonderful world and everything in it: the
teeming tide of time with its reasons to live
and love; to see and hear, to hope and to
pray, and the seasons. Thank heaven. My
greeting senses see and hear how beauty
abounds. As for life with all its broken
dreams, the shining summer sun will
continue to rise, and as the lilting leaves of
autumn fall, dance their last dance, willing
winter waits, to weather the storm until a
new beginning, when all its youth and yen
and yearning. And we, too, must stand our
ground, dine, dance our last dance and dare
to be whole. Only then can we claim
complete contentment.

A Sonnet of Softening Frost

This earth, and every leafless tree stands still,
And the air, when filled with a breathless hush,
And a silence lingering in the bush
Is softly saying, "Look before the till
This icy land of wonder, yours to fill."
A vision of pure whiteness lay in lush,
An even blanket tossed beneath the rush,
And drapes of web with frost on shrub and sill.
For the eyes that see this charm awaking,
And as calm and outline sketch endeavour,
A treasure of gems are in the making
So, with clicking image mind, however,
And a final scan before forsaking.
For as it came, it will go, as ever.

Oz Hardwick   (York)

Snow

In the apology of snow there are no clear statements, only the ambiguity of melting. Whilst sticking resolutely to the facts of light and temperature, it equivocates on colour and intentions. Today it is blue-white, but tomorrow? We'll see.

Beneath these transitory blankets, she loses – or gains – shape. Why can't something, just this one time, be easy to define? A simple statement or a simple outline. A straight tongue that doesn't slip to ice. She moves like an irregular white pulse, fevered and restless. She cannot settle.

Outside, flakes drift in tired waves. Since abandoning sky, they have lost all certainty, become unconvinced by their union with earth, tar and gravel, sceptical of the wisdom of whiteness. They recall water but do not wish to return.

A thin light makes its perfunctory entrance, not assertive enough to wake her, but bathing her form in a hospital glow. If, at some unspecified time later today, she remembers her dreams, they will lack shape or certainty. There will be something about snow, something about deception, and a sense of something important happening just out of sight. There will be colours, but they will be sly, subtle and shifting before they admit to naming.

Don't look outside. Stay here where it is sheltered, if not actually warm. It is not for us to know this day or to judge the truths and lies of snow. Stay here with shadow and light's grudging intrusion. See, she is waking; a Snow Queen slowly unmelting from blankets to bare white flesh.

Later, when she pulls on her name and warm clothing, she will perhaps clear the path. Or perhaps she will skate across yesterday's streams. It all depends. For now, she just concentrates hard on trying not to melt.

Oz Hardwick   (York)

Innamorati
for Jean Cocteau

The maid and the fisherman, drinking in the sun,
lips lapping kisses from cloudless sky,
thighs entwined, tanned ankles,
cottonwhite and candystriped, primary colours
of private carnival, far from lines
of neat houses, theatrically swooning,
raising aloft a glittering glass,
his hand cupping her generous breast,
she wide-eyed in salt-clear air,
soft in plumping lap, almost
dancing to his wavesong whispers:

Come with me to the ocean deep,
To the pull and drift of the dreaming deep,
Lie amongst my nets with starfish at your breast,
With your mermaid hair and your sand-pale breast.
I will taste you, I will toast you with passion-red wine,
And we will rock on the rolling sea, the sea,
We will rock on the rolling sea.

The beached boat, the creel on the quay,
kisses cast like lines, promises and persuasion
drawing the catch to taut arms,
tanned and strong, head thrown back
in song, the land liquefied to waves
in the Mediterranean sun, the maid
sighs, the fisherman sighs, the sea
sighs and whispers: *Come with me.*

Ray Hearne   *(Rotherham)*

Scales in the Key of an April Morning

water tanks clanking at 7 am
a hot shower's clamorous thanksgiving hymn

pipes in the cock-loft extemporize
bridges of assuredly civilised sighs

a daughter's affirmative hair-dryer hum
the radiator's equilibrium

a kettle picks up the melody's thread
butterable moments as yet unspread

frissons from late night unisons blare
out garlic-psalms in the double-glazed air

radio news reports augment
a sense of self-satisfied dissent

pink-loud blossoms amongst resonant creams
heighten a conservatory's tone-deaf dreams

the voluble privet's emphatic group-hug
a subtler hawthorne's quizzical shrug

yellowish flashes of bluetit feathers
a snatch of arpeggio escaping tethers

glints from the green of a tomcat's eye
a light-shows for those about to die

early worm's spasmings, a thrush's trill
conjugations of the verb "to kill"

clouds in cowls black as Fallujah
scowl their dirge to yesterday's future

embellishing those undeposited notes
not stuck already in our children's throats

Ray Hearne   *(Rotherham)*

Flagging

As the train decants passengers
at Sandall and Aggbrigg
a clacker of flung stones
spatter the skin of the windows

a gaggle of kids flagging
from bushes outside the station
Punch and Judy mouthings
gob-hole expletives recycling

a sneer of convulsed faces
bends again to reload
as the guard in bewilderment dithers
I stand at the locked door to dare them

a second volley pits the glass
at bridge-of-nose level
"that's what you call intelligence!
get their bloody arses kicked!"

Voices along the carriage
are exposed in the sun-smutted air
"Stop it now I said...stop it!"
The guard overhears his own pleading.

Three old blokes and a dog
a middle-aged woman and me;
what's left from the atomised mass
of my fabulous working class.

(Ray is well-known as a poet/singer-songwriter/ performer, and was a joint host with Rony Robinson, on Radio Sheffield's "Write-On" poetry programme (sadly missed!). He is also a senior manager for the WEA in the Yorkshire & Humberside region.
He recently released a second CD of his songs, via "Northern Music". Titled "The Wrong Sunshine", it is available from Web sites such as Play.com, or from Ray himself. Enquiries can be directed to Carillon Magazine - address in the front pages.

Ann Heath   (York)

Library Pictures

We put the kettle on and watch the bombs that fall
on Micklegate, vacant shapes that drop and fade
into the pavement with the fags and dust and all
down Cinder Street graffiti splashes mark the dead
edge space of sniper's ally, each tag an alien stain;
we keep our heads down, hurry past; our city walls
blast outwards, warm Tadcaster limestone rains
around us, buries shrapnel in our homes, our schools,
our so-safe lives, while all along the Acomb Road
an army dies inside its smouldered tanks; the dusk
comes fast upon us, green-tinged, night-sighted, strobed
and blind with tracer trails, and still, we wait for doves.

Since every piece of glass has cracked into a fly's
eye, we watch the story unfold endlessly,
and cannot care; a war grinds on; a country dies;
the dispossessed crowd round; nothing new to see,
just something to ignore. Why even shade our eyes?
We watch the bombs draw closer, make a cup of tea.

Ann Heath   (York)

Walking Round the Castle

Just a son and mother, spending time together,
walking round the castle. This is new-born
winter, silence hangs like a half-drawn
breath, and we chat and charm each other.

He is now the taller. He has to bend
to listen, while I crane and shade my eyes,
almost awkward with the pleased surprise
of this grown man who holds my hand.

I talk about the castle, about this wall
some fool once built to keep a world from changing;
now just the beauty of its stone remaining,
and dwarfed within the city's sprawl.

Nothing real can hope to last for ever.
For now, we're walking round the castle together.

elastic time

months of travel squeezed into one day
have cut me loose and here I drift
high inside my skull
like pollen
while
London clatters past a classic film
I've seen through many times red
bus green man
shot grey
real
I feel
that stranger place
Georgian planes blooming salsa
singing colour crackling fierce with heat
stones
baked I
cling one slip
will split me flip me back
into the vanished point the static past

elastic time

Alan Hurst   (Rotherham)

School Life 2007

I enjoy my school life in every way:
A time to laugh, work and play...
But what is that he is pulling out of his pocket?
It's certainly not a five-pound note from his wallet.
He looks straight into my eyes, grim and tense.
What is he seeking here? definitely not recompense.
My gaze will not leave the movement of his hand,
For I cannot see what is in view.
Is it a pen, a pencil, or a you-know-what-who?
His hand draws out the item in question.
He laughs and sniggers,
Banging it on the underside of the table...
It's a knife, a dagger, not just something from a children's fable.

Alan Hurst   (Rotherham)

Lost

I feel I am in a maze
Somewhere in time and space -
No-one to the rescue...
Just more time and space

My life has become a daze
Where seeing and hearing happens only in this maze
I have lost my way...
Please listen to the words I say.

The maze is closing in on me -
Feelings suggest no way out:
So I bang down with my feet...
With a huge scream and shout.

When you find me I will be fine:
Found forever not just for good.
I still haven't found my way out -
But in the end I will - let there be no doubt.

Peter Johnson   (Burley-in-Wharfedale)

The Adverb's Lament

Sadly, bizarrely,
incomprehensibly,
I am now considered
an undesirable,
persona non grata.
I am a self-indulgence,
one to be eschewed
in the earnest pursuit
of more muscular prose.
It would seen there can be
no room for me
in a sentence which seeks
muscularity;
no place in a world
tyrannically ruled
by the noun and the verb
who roundly refuse
to be modified.

Subject and predicate,
totally, comprehensively
unadorned,
is the orthodoxy now.
Tragically,
no need for me and my kind,
who, bitterly, mournfully find
we are cruelly consigned
to a dictionary
of archaic terms.

Peter Johnson   (Burley-in-Wharfedale)

Table Talk

We were chatting,
over dinner, of this and that -
what we thought of the latest
iPod, whether the Algarve was really
all it was cracked up to be,
debating the merits
of wind farms and GM crops,
whether Miranda and Jeff
should go in for IVF,
and my thoughts drifted back
to memories of Grandpa Jack,
who biked it to the Works,
forty years Monday to Friday,
excepting Wakes Week,
and went as far as the Gardeners Arms
of an evening.
And Granny Beatrice,
Empress of the domestic realm,
washing on Mondays, baking Tuesdays,
as far as the High Street for produce
of a Wednesday,
And Chapel on Sundays, the both.
And as we discussed
whether Disneyland was better
in Florida or Paris,
and where would we be without SatNav,
I couldn't help wondering
whatever had they found to talk about.

Pauline Kirk   (York)

Night Call

"You're rubbish!"

In amazement I stared at the phone. " Who's there?" I asked.

"Someone who writes a lot better than you."

I expected to hear Dad was dying. Instead, some nutter was saying my play was no good. I would have slammed the phone down, but the voice was vaguely familiar.

"Who are you?" I persisted.

There was no reply, just laughter. It sounded bitter. We played a grotesque game, waiting to see who would speak first.

Finally the voice began again. "Wouldn't you like to know?" it asked. I could hear music in the background, and muffled giggling - adult giggling. That was more unnerving than threats.

"You think you're so clever," the voice continued. "Standing there, talking drivel about how the cast had done it all. You couldn't construct a brick wall."

The speaker had been at the first night. They knew me. From their tone, they were not rational. I began to feel scared. My number was ex-directory. They probably knew where I lived.

I tried persuasion. They could be a writer themselves, jealous at my success - if you can call a five day run at the local Rep, success.

"The theatre's so unpredictable," I replied. "Your best work gets nowhere, and the silly sketch runs for weeks. One of yours will make it sometime. You're pretty good."

"You bet I am! But I don't sleep around."

"Nor do I," I said coldly.

There was definitely a Canadian accent, but I didn't know anyone from Canada. Presumably my tormentor could act. I thought I could hear a male voice in the background. It seemed to be saying, 'Give it up!'

"Try sending your work to Jan Kennet at the Rep," I suggested. "He's looking for talent."

It was the wrong thing. There was an explosion of foul air at the other end. I slammed the phone down.

It rang again, five minutes later. For a long time I tried to ignore it, but Mum could be calling. As carefully as if I was handling a scorpion, I picked up the handset.

"Not asleep yet?" the voice asked. "Writing another masterpiece?" "Get lost!" I shouted.

It was impossible to sleep now, but I lay down and tried. Then I thought of the answerphone. If I put that on, Mum, or the hospital, could contact me. Recording an insult would feel silly.

The anwerphone wasn't working. I had forgotten. I was going to get myself a new phone, one of those modern ones that showed the caller's number. If I had got round to it, I'd know who was plaguing me now. Cursing my stupidity, I went back to bed.

It was nearly an hour before the phone rang again, and for every minute my nerves were waiting.

The voice was definitely more slurred. "I tried sending stuff to Jan," it said, unannounced. "He sent it back. Didn't even include a note. "There was no music now, or male voice. The speaker seemed to be alone. "But then I don't have your 'special relationship'," she added suddenly.

I still could not work out who was speaking. My dressing gown was too thin for a winter's night, and I was shivering. "I don't have any special relationship," I said, only to feel angry with myself. "It wouldn't be your business if I did," I added.

It sounded so lame. Furiously I put down the phone.

There were no more calls until six o'clock. Perhaps my night caller had fallen asleep, dead drunk or recovering from whatever high she favoured. I began to feel sorry for her.

Compassion evaporated when I got the last call. "I'm doing myself in, you know," the voice said, quite calmly. "Topping myself. It'll be your fault." Then the line went dead.

For a full minute I stared in horror. Then I tried to walk away. It was the ultimate bullying threat, the "You'll be sorry" technique. The trouble was, it could be true.

Shivering in the hall, I stared at the phone, willing it to ring. Nothing happened.

Finally my mind cleared. There was a number I could ring to check the last caller. My mind was too stupid with sleep and emotion to remember it, so I had to fumble through the directory. I could hardly turn the pages.

As soon as the automated voice spoke, I understood.

Urgently I dialled, but there was no answer. Putting the phone down, I tried to think what to do. By the time I had driven round there, it could be too late. Magda was not the sort to make threats lightly, even when she was on the vodka and coke.

I doubt if she appreciated me sending an ambulance, but then, what are colleagues for?

Patrick Lodge   (York)

Sandwiches at the Seaside

Rain falling like gauze
dressings, through which
sky and shore seep together,
promiscuous as unveined blood;
drizzled too are the figures,
embossed in bas-relief, against

the concrete shelter walls:
gothic in the mock doric.
Imagine father, mother, me
in pac-a-macs, blue-creased
like engineering drawings;
motionless in down-mouthed

tableau, sorbing regret.
Sandwiches, salad, slabcake,
thermos; tupperwared milk,
sugar, salt, teaspoons too.
Meticulous commissary toil
of beach–going, slowly leaching

joy from the expectation of
this day; each leaf unfurled,
each tomato sliced, each bread
square spread, a cumulation
of cloud occluding the dwarf
white sun in the foremilk sky;

Slub in the shimmer-silk rain, we
are poor people at the seaside,
wearing this day as a sodden
overcoat, watching returning
buses, replete, sluice by,
the life within forever opaque.

Patrick Lodge   (York)

Bungee Resurrection

Over St Sampson's Square bells peal into an empty sky;
a slatted steel spider rig broods above four trampolines,
floating lily pads on a yorkstone pond. From a cats-cradle
of pulleys, guys, pillars, hang bungee ropes, blue and yellow

lianas trailing across this urban jungle - the tools of translation
from earth to sky. A boy boasts to a pretty blonde girl
how high he can bounce, how he can dance easy between
pavement and tree tops. Transfigured in sunlight he walks

the air currents; he demonstrates to us all his
backflips, rolls, tucks and somersaults: doubles, triples
ringing out clear and high above the plane trees.
His clapper legs unbound kick out in joy. He sinks down

on the cave –black rubber paten, pauses an eternity, swings
up, rising, arms outspread, haloed in treetop light,
all eyes follow his ascending; the blonde girl walks away.

York Writers

We are a friendly group of people
who meet on
alternate Wednesdays
at The Yorkshire Terrier,
Stonegate, York
at
8pm

Chairman: Clint Wastling
e-mail: clint01@madasafish.com
Web: http://www.yorkwriters.org.uk

Ian Lowery   (Huddersfield)

Dampened Ego

Today the dawn is as gloomy as it is unlikely,
For a soulful lunar passage has obscured the whole
With slippery trails which dominate the very morning's perfume
And the parts of what were before are no more,
And the parts of what I was before are no more.

The tear-stained sun, pathetic and numb,
Has ducked its pallor behind waspish shrouds,
Chased by the same soothing breeze as before,
It refuses to sail as high, rather absorbs the touch
And the parts of what were are deadened to senses.

Yet the same sprite flutters around me like a cloak
And refuses to let the swell subside
Below the tide line where
The shredded shadows of perceived clarity
Hitch a ride on the ghost of yesterday's gear.

Ian Lowery   (Huddersfield)

Revived Ego

The onlookers flesh skulked
As her cocked index scooped from the bubbling pot,
Crossed lips which bore the scars of hardship,
Bore the smoke of Fetatti's violated sarcophagus,
And brush the lips from blue to purple...to scarlet.
As the heat rose, the onlookers flesh slinked;
Their idea of hot was five degrees,
And of cold, three.
As the heat rose from her mantra
Their lungs confine a nascent catalyst
To awaken that which hovers among the droplets of mist
Low slung over the moorland,
To impassion those spasms below the shroud.
With the blood rush pumping in their ears,
The onlookers retreat in unison into their cowls
...then start to hoist.
As the cocked index provoked her bubbling pot,
The onlookers slithered inside
Their hoods of comfort,
Their swathes of veil.
As the heat rose from inside,
So did their awakened mantra,
So long unsung.

These two poems are from Ian's latest work,
"The Little Book of Metaphoric Egos"
a collection of 17 poems as yet unpublished

Steve Mawson   (Rotherham)

Go Fish

There was a time while married to Emily, where it was as though we were playing 'Go Fish'.

My little sister and I had played the game on rainy days at the seaside. When we were at the caravan, we never prepared for rainy days. So inevitably, we would spend the afternoon peering at each other over playing cards held to our chest.

'Got any kings?' I would ask, while trying to spy her cards reflected in the television screen.

'Go Fish!' she would tell me with a silly grin.

And for a time, that is how it became with Emily and I. The rainy days had come and we were not prepared. When I really needed her, she was too busy. No matter how much I tried to show her my cards, no matter how much of myself I gave to her, she had to keep her secrets. She was telling me to 'Go Fish'. It was this, above all else, that made me want to end things with her.

It was a hot, overcast day in August when I asked her to meet me at our favourite cafe in town, to talk. They had a nice outdoor seating area with a little fountain and the waiters wore little waistcoats that made Emily laugh.

I would wait for the perfect moment to talk about our future. I thought I would recognise it when it came, but it came too quickly, and the words became stuck in my throat. When she put her coffee down and looked at me with raised eyebrows, I was sure she knew.

Over her shoulder, I could see a waiter with over-sculpted hair collecting coffee mugs onto his tray. I found him very distracting. I wanted to look everywhere besides straight at Emily. But when the waiter flicked his fringe away, something landed on his tray, flipping it out of his hands sending mugs crashing to the ground.

'Jesus,' he cried, and looked down.

Everyone put down his or her Skinny Lattes and Grande Ice-Teas and stared. At his feet was a small tropical fish, flipping its tail and gobbling the air.

People further away craned their necks to see what we were all looking at. The waiter glanced over his shoulder, trying to see who had thrown this animal at him when another fish landed on the table next to us. It landed neatly in a half-full cup of Mocha with Foam.

My mouth was still open, ready to deliver the message that I had struggled with for weeks but Emily had her back to me then as she pointed to another fish that had landed in a woman's handbag.

I closed my mouth. Thousands of exotic fish began to rain from the sky.

Everyone in the café forecourt kicked away from their chairs and ran for cover. A woman screamed when a fish landed in her hair and beat against her ear. As she ran into the café, she collided with a tall man who was nursing a Grande Cappuccino in a paper cup. The hot coffee sprayed its owner in the face causing more cries of pain. Across the road, a courier on a pushbike skidded into a bush, as the falling fish became a slippery silver carpet.

Emily and I dived into a neighbouring antique shop that had large windows. I could smell fish in the air and we could hear people sobbing in the café.

Emily was laughing, 'What the hell is this?'

For the second time I opened my mouth to speak and discovered I could produce no words.

The shop owner had come to the window and leaned against a large piece of driftwood that had been fashioned into a totem pole, 'Well I never,' he said, 'Raining fish!'

People were running and slipping and falling, others were taking cover under shop fronts and bus stops. Traffic stopped dead. And as quickly as it started, it stopped. More people started to cry.

I turned to Emily who was smiling at the shop owner. He too wore the same grin.

'This is completely bizarre,' I said 'How are you two so calm?'

The shopkeeper began walking amongst his antiques and said, 'It's just one of those things. You can't prepare for it, but there's no need to panic.'

That evening as I lay beside Emily in bed, I could not decide what had been stranger, the fish raining from the sky, or the shopkeeper who took it in his stride. I never did speak to Emily about breaking up, and I am glad I did not.

Rainy days come and we are not always prepared. But, like the shopkeeper said, there's no need to panic.

Julie Mellor   (Penistone)

Dates

Her spine curves to a question mark
as she leans over the desk, tracking lives
through books borrowed and returned.

The computer signals an overdue, beeps
like the flat line on a heart monitor.
The man who reads free newspapers

looks her way, nods and smiles.
She's stuck in this job like a fly on paper,
watches the seasons pass beyond

the plate glass window, sees her reflection,
thinner than she was at twenty.
The floor is a grid of carpet tiles,

curled at the edges like stale bread.
The newspaper reader pushes back his chair,
goes to buy coffee from the machine.

She gave up coffee years ago; it's bad
for the heart. She hates his obscure requests,
trawling through the stack for local history books

long out of print, the urine-smell of pages
starved of air. He asked her out once,
to see a film. She made an excuse.

Being single has become a way of life,
like mending torn pages and chasing fines.

(Winner in Rotherham Arts' 2009 "Mike Haywood" competition)

Signposts Writing Development Project

Working in South Yorkshire with writers and writing groups.

Signposts Writing Development Project is an arts organisation that runs writing projects and activities. We are also one of the main information providers in South Yorkshire, through *The Inky* (Newsletter) and our Writers Resource Centre, where we can supply information about writing activities, groups, events and organisations in Sheffield and South Yorkshire.

Writers Resource Centres: advice and information.

The Inky Writers Newsletter: Free to subscribe to.

Workshops and Projects: Details via the Inky.

Young Writers Groups: Aged 13 - 18 & 19 - 25.

For more information or to subscribe to the Inky:

Email: info@signpostssouthyorks.org.uk

Web: http://www.signpostsonline.org

Phone: 0114 2536722

Signposts Writing Development Project

The Circle

33 Rockingham Lane

Sheffield, S1 4FW

Susan Mary Morgan   (Barugh Green, Barnsley)

The Poppy Field

Just by chance I turned to look:
Such joy! I gazed in awe;
A hundred thousand poppies
A hundred thousand more.

Blood red on the horizon
A blazing field, I saw
This patchwork quilt of colour,
A hundred thousand more.

This feast of fiery poppies
I'm sure weren't there before,
Swaying in the gentle breeze,
A hundred thousand more.

If I could paint this picture
Sheer pleasure to restore,
Stand proud in all their glory,
A hundred thousand more.

Man shamed this crimson beauty
On the bloody field of war!
A hundred thousand poppies,
A hundred thousand more.

Susan Mary Morgan   *(Barugh Green, Barnsley)*

Eggshells

Looking back
on the whole rigmarole
of courting and cavorting,
love, honour, always obey,
wet sex and endless passion
as mundane life ticked on,
walking on air became walking on eggshells
as jealousy seeped in.
Hating his obsession with possession,
slowly the fire went out.
Love now hard and cold
useless
as the band of gold.

An Honourable Sport

On a green expanse lined with chalk, towering poles dominate
this honourable sport. Legions of warriors tramp the earth with
studded feet, bodies braced, opponents faced, chanting rituals
now complete. The game is on. Passing, dashing, charging,
pumping testosterone, raging bulls driving through, engage,
crouch, tussle, wrestle, to keep possession of the leather trophy.
A sickening thud as bodies clash with beetroot faces and spiky
legs. The ground shudders as crumpled men disentangle from a
heap of spit and sweat. Boys turn into men at the sound of a
whistle. This is a sport for warriors, disciplined and fearless. A
run charged with rocket fuel brings knuckle-cracking excitement,
as the crowd roars, the final try...Game over, the battle fought,
hand- shaking, back-patting and
applause. Congratulations, commiserations, for this honourable
sport.

Daithidh MacEochaidh   (Hebden Bridge)

Sun In the Grass

Even by you, the park by the Vltava,
your head in my lap, the spot of sun,
filtered through the leaves of the tree above,
heats your hair, turns its colour,
your head in my lap,
hearing the discourse of strangers,
the burr of water, passing,
even here, by you,
the smell of sun, your woven hair,
I miss the grey morning wet
of the Teifi, its wan reeds
its greening of soft mud
the slow song broken
in the long staggered meander of quiet impotence,
draining to the estuary, lost to the sea;
the gentle weight of your head,
in my lap, the warm breath against my skin,
the Vltava moving on, the smell of sun
in your hair, avoiding all talk,
we listen to the discourse of strangers;
            search for shades of empathy.

Daithidh MacEochaidh   (Hebden Bridge)

A Pause of Flood

On the second day of storm
turgid with words most trite
the idiotic bloat and boast
of the poetic in the wind and grass
declaring that here the blades
of rushes cut the wind - the
futility of an over alembicated
praise. The sting is always invisible,
tearing the whipped reeds from
their beds, thrown to water, their
ripped tongued, dumb drowning,
the cut of the wind an unvoiced
ache. I long for you in the green
rushes and brown. In the soft land
giving to sea-strengthened water,
the broken river's mouth. I seek
the memory of words we chewed
together, sucked dry, their savour
out, hockling out granules of letters
amongst the emptied shells of estuarine
sand, the greed of embittered need.

On the second day of storm
the wind was left to carry
all the dead words I'd kept
warm in the mouth that no
longer finds the cut of your
lips. I long for you in
the green rushes and brown.

*(Daithidh is the editor of Skrev Press.
http://www.skrevpress.com
See final page)*

Andy McMaster (Retford)

Fred

Little old man on a wet lonely road turns off to walk up a path in the park called Gensing Gardens. And the wet soaks through the formal flower beds, through the informal shrub borders wherein he'll be found five days a week, keeping the place utility, matter of fact clean.

Let's view a little closer as he treks up that steep slope inclining towards his hut, tucked away in the protective, hiding evergreens. He planted them when they were but adolescent trees, needing care. He planted all you'll see, with a little help, either side of the green-lined way, way up to the hut. Now that's really something to view. Once you have, you'll remember it always: leaf-laden gardener's hideaway, little old elongated brick and asbestos hut cluttered full of inter-seasonal gardening gear. Gadgets, no... They can't be called anything but Fred's, for the "forks border" and "spades border" are all the sharp steel warmer, all the shinier sharp-edged, tell a tale a tool of old times: fifteen years and a little more service with our Fred, who doesn't look a day over fifty I sometimes tell him, and sometimes tell him he does. He looks well about that time of life...

Bent about the shoulders, a leathery kind of face, wrinkled by rain, wind and late-night pints. And as well as trying to gain his own weight in liquid refreshment, his eyes do not tire from refreshing all the folk who come into the park. You'd think he never owned a watch, he never wears one. His trusty stomach, the park people, and an empty Park Drive packet - they tell him when it's time, when tools should take a break: tools can always lean by themselves. But you wouldn't think that if you worked with Fred. However, enough of that, the Foreman's coming.

Andy McMaster   (Retford)

Mist Over Morton Farm

Fine new day And early August:
not a human sound but the magical half-light wrapped around
the farm cluster. Trees silhouette above encircling mist,
their forms clearer by the minute

Only a few heavy bales remain on the cornfield of yesterday,
brooding darkly on their forgotten lot.
Cockerel calls time out as the first buildings shy out of the mist.
Cool breeze now and mist slips thin away.

First birds beyond wound-up cockerel quietly, gently sound out
the hedgerows. First car on auto pilot:
half-awake driver is more than half glad to be here.
We, only two human beings in sight and sound in complete accord.

In Summer

All is content now, at midday with a sky of long awaited blue.
A mouse cuts the kernel of a nut, hazel here already.
A blackbird scolds he who dares to greedy-eye her nest:
quiet, the interloper gone. Train bound for human things
passes through and allows back the silence.

Trees full-leafed rejoice by a keening thank you to the wind and rain
a summer song for the good trading between incandescent insects
                                                              and flowers.
Blackbirds wet and sun wood sing full-throated happiness after
                                                              showers.
Field lark fountains a hover of trilling joy.
God looks on and forgets his sadness.

Steven Nash   (York)

Bearing Witness

Death has no eyes; no need for the
sunglasses Orpheus offers
but in the amber hour, as night
succeeds day, he sees everything.

Remember your birth? You were there
flapping on your back like a fresh-
caught cod, eyes squinting, blinded
by the blood you'd shared a last time.

In strange churches Belgrade's Masters
wore blindfolds as they pawed chess pieces
to the hostile therapy of
a thunderstorm - Knight to Queen Four.

Remember the Spartan woman?
The cottage? The tree trunk? The skunks?
If that tree had a name
you did not care to know it.

Only Romeo and Juliet
know what occurred in the crypt,
when dark could not come soon enough
to embrace and lay the blade deep.

Remember the unshackling
of the siren's hiss through the snow?
Dog-tongued and apron-strung
always leaning to follow.

Open the charred and forgotten grave
to discover only fish
hooks still waiting to be something,
broken, charred always inexact.

Steven Nash (York)

Taking the Long Way Home
(in memory of Kelly Roxanne)

Sitting on sand spread too thin over rock
I watch our old friends as they clash with the waves.
They perch crouched and glistening only to fall
from their boards, then from the water they break
upwards into sky, taking deep gulps of the day.
They are so far; they look so small.

If you were here we'd embarrass them all,
digging for fraggles whilst they showed their moves.
The entire beach would be your playground and no stares
could stop you dancing, or singing back the gulls calls.
They raise beckoning waves in arcs and loops,
send pleas to join them upwards as flares.

But I've got to write a paragraph,
picking at the years with a fingernail
hoping for just a little blood; like when you
said you couldn't find poetry in Sylvia Plath;
the only real poems were fairytales;
that no one wrote anything new.

Tonight we'll fill the coastline with your songs,
with lies, with stories, with beer-skewed memories
and tomorrow we'll follow the shoreline's foam,
just as you and I always did after those long
nights playing dives, huddled against the breeze,
always taking the long way home.

(Steven Nash is a teacher currently doing research for a Phd, but (quote) "earns his keep as a (kind of) musician playing to anyone foolish enough to stay in the bar")

Marion New   (Oxspring, Sheffield)

A Backward Glance

A grey love in two chairs
you with the remote.
This isn't the whole truth,
the alpha and omega,
we've travelled to places
that only explorers found.

Back to a time of tension,
tempers and a heavy load.
Now change the tune
to music and choices.
Then we are middle-aged orphans
when parents leave with daughters.

A journey of children and babies,
birth with fingers and toes.
The smile on my face as I walk
up the aisle two minutes early
and walk down again to our
first date a few hours late.

"What's on?"
"Shall we go to the pictures?"

Marion New   (Oxspring, Sheffield)

Train's Late

I saw a heron last night,
he stood in grey light
that was giving up the day.
Rain slashed diagonally
against windows.
The train crawled across the bridge,
people bent in the rain.
He didn't.
He was straight and still
in the wet.

Keith Newing   (Rotherham)

Burlington Blackbird and Hen

Lordly blue blackbird, in spring song,
With cigar in wing,
Yellow beak a puffing and gold-tipped cane,
Monocled wincing eye,
Black velvet topper,
On a flutter from Mayfair,
Windswept and clicked feathers a dashing
Black flying cape and brief case.
In a hurry to West One.
A Lord so noble.
Heart of London.
Black wings, umbrella fanned,
Sheltering a pink bonneted hen,
Who sings, in reply to a lord, a warm rosy cuddling tune.
Burlington blackbird with lady.
Down street, swaying, swaggering, full of bubbles and burping.
Claw scratching in mid air.
Angered flapping wing slaps and tussling in argumentative and
                                                    charging flurries.

Toff Burling blackbird.
For a passing fragrant cloud of mine,
Together wing in wing, down walking stick stride of Burlington
                                                    arcade.

All for pounds in flicked sterling.

Keith Newing   (Rotherham)

War and Peace

War is lunacy,
Peace is sanity.

War is folly,
Peace is joy.

War is hell,
Peace is a calming church bell.

War is the wrong way,
Peace is the right way.

Fly

Buzzy, whizzy, fuzzy fly,
Buzzing before my crossed eye.

Buzzy, whizzy, fuzzy fly,
Landing on my tie.

Buzzy, whizzy, fuzzy fly,
Fly food am I.

Buzzy, whizzy, fuzzy fly,
Buzzing all around on by.

David Norris-Kay   *(Sheffield)*

Considering a Leaf
(For June White)

Evokes a filament of youth
where sunray paints a summer wood
with dappled patterns of the past
which never can be understood.

Too complex patterns, shadows black,
are laid along our serried fears,
and in this leaf I see them traced
like veins of lifeblood through the years.

Such shadowed fears make us alive,
and mixed with joy, life anthems sing
that from each Autumn's sad decay
awakes a seed of certain spring.

Swan

White ghost glides on the darkened mere,
With graceful neck coiled in space,
In peace that knows no inward fear,
She leaves a wake of laughing lace.

In rolling ripple's dancing moon,
A cygnet seeks her preening queen,
Who wakes a sylvan-piper's tune
That floats through glades of living green.

The slow span of her spreading wings,
Flings splashing stars on seas of night:
And where their breeze-borne echo rings,
The spectral swan will pass from sight.

*("Swan" won 3rd prize in the Coast-to-Coast
international writing competition 2007)*

David Norris-Kay   (Sheffield)

Sonnet: Roses
(In memory of fellow poet Margaret Munro Gibson)

Where tumbled tors shadowed a stone-walled field,
And hostile aircraft skimmed encircling skies,
You showed determination not to yield,
To enemies of reason and their lies -
Like thorny briars creeping all around,
That pricked your conscience with a sterner view
Of England in her peril, then you found
A clearer way where storm clouds broke anew:
Sudden shafts of sunshine warmed the briar,
And inspiration slowly came to bloom,
You found yourself within a softer shire,
Where peace, at last, suffused a restful room.

   Your words, like roses, blossomed from past strife,
   Composing verses of a worthwhile life.

(Margaret served her country as height finder
for heavy anti-aircraft guns [Ack Ack] in 1942)

David's poems are included in his book ,From Time-Buried Years,
a collection of 61 poems about childhood, the natural world, and
passing time.. ISBN 978-0-9553589-7-5
Published by Indigo Dreams Publishing and available for £7.99
from the publisher or from David himself.

Muriel Noton   (North Anston, Sheffield)

Rain

The child stumbled to the window. She was cold in her skimpy dress, and the bare floorboards were icy to her feet. She tried to rub a space on the grimy pane to investigate the noise which had disturbed her from a deeply troubled sleep.

It was the rain. A sudden storm had sent heavy drops scudding and pounding into the narrow alleyway beneath her window, bouncing across the cobbles which shone in the light of the lone street lamp. She stared, wondering, still half asleep. The rain was steadying into a downpour, but even the dirt on the glass could not completely obscure the shafts of pure silver driven across the lamplight. A thin slice of sky visible over the roofs was black - black with the storm clouds but black because it was midnight.

She was alone in the house, locked in this squalid room. There was an old mattress on the floor with an ancient blanket, a plate caked with remains of some unidentifiable meal and a cup. The dim light was from the street lamp; there was no source of warmth this winter's night. Her face, streaked with tears long since shed, was bemused by the uneasy sleep from which the sound of the rain had aroused her.

Opposite across the alley was an old brick wall, part of a derelict building, a warehouse or something similar. As the rain was blown against it the water seeped downwards, forming to an imaginative mind patterns of fingers and hands stretching out and moving, continually moving.

She shuddered.

The wind shook the door to her room, and the small girl turned quickly, fear in her eyes now. Was that the dreaded heavy step on the landing? The rattle of a key in the lock? She watched the door handle in the dim light, tensed as a frightened animal, but it did not turn and she gradually relaxed.

She turned back to the window and was fascinated by the spouting water from a broken pipe draining from the roof nearby, a temporary waterfall gushing in full flood down to the ground below. But now the wind had changed slightly and the rain was falling against her own window, a hissing cascade of silver-grey further obscuring her view. Thus she could only just make out a heap of rubbish in a doorway on the alley floor which suddenly moved to reveal a bent and scarecrow-like figure which shook a fist at the sky and wandered away, leaving a cardboard-box bed and a pile of old bits of clothing and sodden newspaper.

66

"Tatty-man," the girl whispered, and her breath clouded the glass. She knew him, the down-and-out; he was a regular in the alley and had sometimes waved to the pale little face peering through the high window. Once he had blown a kiss: she remembered that, and she rubbed furiously at the pane to watch him meander out of sight. But he had never enquired about her or tried to help even though he knew something was very wrong there. He kept his own counsel, which experience had taught him to do. He had enough worries of his own he reckoned.

Now the rain was petering out. A few drops spattered against the window and the drainpipe's flow dwindled. There was a brief spell of pale moonlight between the torn clouds, and the storm was over. The girl sighed and wandered back to her bed. She pulled the blanket over her shoulders and fell asleep. Would her dreams be the usual ones of cold and dirt and sadness, deprivation and abuse, or would her imagination after the rain lead her to magic lands of crystal waterfalls, knights with silver lances, and ragged gypsies who turned out to be princes in disguise?

(Muriel is the Secretary of "The Scribblers",
a writing group based in North Anston and Harthill, Nr Sheffield)

Julia Pearson   (Silkstone, Sheffield)

Bottles and Jars

Seething in the darkness stands the angry furnace
Hunger in its belly, spitting white hot flames
Guzzling the cullet and the ground-down limestone
Urgent amber liquid boiling in its veins

Eager for the feeding there's a row of hungry robots
Swallowing the nectar as it slips down the line
Sculpting, shaping, relentless, mechanical
Creators, dictators of intelligent design

Ram-rods and pistons bathed in oily blackness
Practising dexterity, collecting every gob
Mindless, yet mindfully, they turn and blow and pinch and push
Delivering the bottles with a pride in every job

Out into the cool zone for testing and packaging
Lines and lines of bottles standing waiting in the queue
Jostling and shuffling past the faceless examiner
Anxious for the verdict: just the flawless will get through

Manoeuvring the regiments, the soulless automata
Boxes up the bottles and assembles all the jars
Piles them up in cages gathered in the corner
And sends them to the warehouse for dispatch to near and far

Travelling the world by lorry and container ship
Clinking empty vessels, expecting to be filled
With medicines and marmalade, condiments and beetroot
Olive oil or pale ale, best served chilled

Stacked and shelved in supermarkets, purchased for their contents
Taken home and emptied, washed and left to drain
Carefully collected, sorted, recycled
Returning to the furnace they begin their lives again

Waiting in the darkness still, the angry furnace
Hunger in its belly, spitting white hot flame

Julia Pearson   (Silkstone, Sheffield)

Firstborn, Now Twenty-One

In shock, I held you, melting, falling
Eyes so deep and berry black
Hungry fingers touched exploring
Velvet flesh so cushion soft
Deepest instincts, fractured night times
Forging bonds and vows unsaid
Living calmly every moment
Fragile dreams danced on ahead
Now you stride out, towering, eager
Now, life starting, carefree, strong
Glimpses of the child behind you
In the past where we belong
       Still in shock I watch with joy
       The complete man who was the boy.

Graham Rippon   (Brinsworth, Rotherham)

Visitors Are Good For Business

It was the day that Sam the donkey died that Dad decided to open a tea shop, or rather, to take over the one that closed last year. Its closure had surprised us as it had always seemed busy. "Amateurs," commented Dad. "Didn't know what they were doing. We'll soon have it up and running at a profit, and it will be much better than lugging donkeys round and round a beach."

Mum was in her private heaven. She'd always dreamed of running a posh hotel or restaurant. "It'll be the Tea Shop of the North," she pronounced with a faraway look in her eye. "People will come from all over the place to taste my tea and toast."

She grabbed pencil and paper. "We'll have to plan it properly, though. Right! Dad - you're the Restaurant Manager and Customer Relations Executive. I'll be the Catering Director and Head Chef. Now, you Kevin, you will be our Finance and Premises Manager."

"Hang on, Mum," I protested, "it's only a thirty-seater sea front coffee bar."

"Don't you want to improve yourself," she retorted. "Better than that Army idea you were talking about last year! You just watch - a few months and we'll be raking it in!"

Yeah, I thought, just like the donkeys: we started with six and now we've got two. I had to admit, however, that there could be compensations: being a Manager was better than being a Donkey Assistant.

Dad sold the donkeys a few days later. I can still hear Mum shrieking at him in the bedroom: "Forty quid! Forty quid! You barnpot! They're worth more than that on a butcher's slab!" This was followed by a hollow clunk. I didn't investigate - blood gives me the collywobbles.

We spent a (borrowed) fortune on refurbishment. There wasn't a wall, door or ceiling that didn't scream for attention. Mum flapped around with advice in between disappearing to admire her new kingdom (or should that be queendom?), otherwise known as the kitchen.

Dad planned and commented and judged. He even held the stepladder once in a while. Me? I slaved from morn till night. "You're built for it," said Dad, clutching his famous bad back.

I suppose he's right seeing that I'm twenty-one, six feet tall and fifteen stone in weight, but I did hanker after the donkeys.
Anyway, on the first day of May, we opened. To my astonishment, we didn't do at all badly that first month. If we hadn't had to recompense one chap because part of the ceiling fell on him and another for a touch of food poisoning, and, of course, the woman who missed her

coach by waiting for two hours to be served, we might even have made a profit.

"Teething troubles," agreed Mum and Dad. "You wait till the holiday season starts properly."

I wasn't looking forward to the holiday season. I'd already lost a stone in weight and Mandy, my fiancée, was threatening to dump me if I didn't take her out soon. Still, there were compensations: with my single month's experience, I was well qualified to get any job on any complaints desk anywhere in the world.

Dad was right. Trade zoomed in June. Dull moments and I became total strangers and I sweated off some more weight.

Somewhere, in the midst of sponging down customers and dousing Mum's chip pan fires, I heard through a friend of a friend that Mandy had got engaged to someone else. Still, there were compensations: at the end of June, profits were marginally ahead of refunds and Dad promised me a wage. We were in business!

Then, on the second Tuesday in July, in the middle of forty cod and chips for a elderly coach party we'd squeezed in with the promise of a discount for crowding, a strange man walked in: a little man with a fierce stride and a sharp pinstripe suit. He had a briefcase in one hand and a fancy badge in the other.

"Public Liability Insurance?" he snapped at my father.

"Eh?" said Dad.

"Music licence?" snarled back the suit.

"Eh? said Dad.

"I want to see your kitchens!" He grabbed Dad by the shoulder and marched him through the swing doors into the perpetual blue haze of Mum's empire.

We were closed within the hour. It was then that Dad decided to take on a polystyrene-carpet cleaning franchise.

Me?

I'm joining a ballet school - I'm thin enough now.

Barbara Robinson   (Boston Spa)

Out Of the Sun

I ran and danced and laughed and sang
down leafy lanes of endless youth,
so happy in my sun-touched skin,
a world of freedom, daisy chains
and childhood dreams in gilded frames.
When schooldays came. I laughed with joy,
new books I treasured, read with awe.
Past deeds now told from days of old
and new lands on mapped pages drawn,
all learnt with heart-felt passion borne.

I had not learned of sorrow then
nor strife, death or sad parting,
and every day I'd laugh and play,
pure happiness along the way.
But the wheels of time grind onwards
to a new world where cares abide,
I have aged, grown melancholy,
those young days have now sadly died.
For in adult life I am tamed,
my spirit curbed, my laughter culled
as though my life now dulled should be
an epitome of straight-laced ways.
And how I miss those childhood days.

Barbara Robinson *(Boston Spa)*

Life's Orchestra

Comes early dawn when overture of day
plays gently on sweet harps of sylvan breeze,
caresses foxgloves and a dew-kissed lawn
then softly chants amongst the leafy trees.
Lark sings a solo, high piccolo notes
and chaffinch duets with a lilting song.
Thrush and Blackbird both trill fine descant,
a glorious cantata from this avian throng.

With broad daylight comes the revving of brass,
trumpeting horns and engines' loud drumming.
Life's movement now rising in crescendo,
the people's choir an incessant humming.
The feral pigeons, swooping, scavenging,
flap wings in time to the orchestral sway.
Until the tempo of day's life pulse slows
dusk waits with patience for its turn to play.

Lovers dance and sway to the evening's beat
as sweet voice sings and guitar softly strums,
then comes a backdrop of deep pink and gold
as lone blackbird pipes in the setting sun.
The heavenly baton will soon come to rest
but there's one more movement still to play.
a celestial fanfare to laud life's heartbeat,
a starlight symphony to close this fine day.

Miles Salter   (York)

Instructions for downloading the human heart

It's easy. All you need
is superfast broadband
and the right chip
harboured in your chest,
nesting between lung and sternum.

Make yourself comfortable.
Attach yourself to the port (the flesh coloured wire)
and slide a credit card
from brown leather.
Wait for 9 hours. Try to stay calm.

There's a graphic you can watch.
As the heart blooms within you,
it fleshes out on screen. Watch it bulge
with life. Hear that thud, keeping time.

Afterwards, our guarantee : your blood
will roll quicker through arteries and veins,
white and red cells motor
through an internal roller coaster.
You'll feel decades shrivel, find
evenings pulse with possibility,
and desert your bed
as the birds proclaim dawn.
Your skin may glow.

One more thing. The heart is merely an engine.
A valve of sorts. All that other stuff
(anger, jealousy, compassion etc)
– all of that is up to you.
Your new heart won't alter those.
Ready now ? Deep breath. Sharp scratch. Here we go.

Miles Salter   (York)

Jade Goody's Face
(The Sun, March 5th 2009)

From the tabloid's barking face
your eyes smash mine.
On the cover of a nearby magazine
your cheeks and eyes are made up, airbrushed.
You're smiling, well lit, as an
abundant life lays itself for the public.

White marquee. Flowers. Security:
these props clutter the stage door
to the busy, chintzy years,
the days you've lived through winking lenses
that stare you down, one click at a time.

And now you're staring me down
through a drama the papers adore,
harbouring your daily minutiae
as if you're everyone's cousin, daughter, friend.
At the end, you won't let the cameras in.

They were there for frivolity,
ignorance, a big wedding.
But some things need secrecy,
and won't be recorded.
The human heart. What's never said.

Your face, tricked to crazy horror, meets my eyes
in the convenience shop. Here's the vicious truth, Jade,
scratching your turbulent insides and halving your vision
the dark, circular pool that hunts you, snapping,
groping your face for a moment's eye contact.

(Miles is the Writer in Residence, at HMP Everthorpe
and Winner, 2009 Sentinel Poetry Competition)

Kerry Louise Sheridan   (Sheffield)

Despair

Despair.
Non-physical in its existence,
but ever-presently there.
Deep-set within the mind
it vibrates within the soul,
consumes you in space and time,
like an enormous black hole.
It dictates the way your think,
how you conduct your way,
and even when you wake with hope
it eventually clouds your day.
Sometimes, you find it hard to deal
with even the simplest things,
and people you thought would care
don't seem to understand the way you feel.
Or so you think.
But they do.
they just can't bear to watch you cry
and, together, they can help you
make life become bright.
You can get there in the end,
though not without a fight
against this illness called Depression.
So you'll still have darker days
But the clouds will go away - you'll see.
Just like me.

Kerry Louise Sheridan   (Sheffield)

For My Love

I love you so much,
Angel of mine.
Your words enriched with sentiment,
Warm kisses - divine.
My heart plays a joyful tune
When you are in my wake;
When your absence is upon me
Longing makes me ache.
Your passionate caress overcomes me,
I feel your touch from within.
It feel so sweet this love so pure -
surely it must a sin.
But, no...
I have you for always
To love and cherish and hold.
Yes, I have you
And you have me,
As together we grow old.

Vic Speight   (Barnsley)

Creativity

To create. To cause to exist. To bring into existence. Therefore I ask you to please consider that to create, is not just confined to excellence in the arts. To paint wondrous pictures, to write scintillating words or to make magnificent music. So my story relates to a creativity in a relationship that is very much out of the ordinary scheme of things.

It was a totally unexpected call, so unexpected that she was able to play the 'guess who' game on the phone. For a few seconds I was at a loss as to whom this pleasant voice belonged to, until, I can't explain why, it dawned on me that it was Sheila who had been on the Paris trip with her husband. But I kept the 'guess who' game going. The game ended with unrestrained laughter from both of us that strangely acted as a kind of release from our inhibitions and we began to talk, to talk of real things, she began by saying how she and her husband had both enjoyed my company in Paris but then - and I don't understand this - her words created in me a comfort; though ordinary words, they were what I wanted to hear, everything she said seemed so right. There were no romantic connotations in our conversation but she had planted something within me and after the call I felt compelled to seek out how and why she had created this feeling I had. Who was she; I mean really; who was she?

Of course we did arrange to meet, we had a pub lunch and again. It happened, all she said was perfectly in accord with how I saw things that mattered. I told her this. She smiled. It was a smile of recognition, of knowing what I was about and said that I had had the same effect on her.

We talked of cabbages and kings, of shoes and ships and sealing wax. We seemed to speak a secret language, a way of saying things that couldn't be said any other way, creating in each other the ability to tell things of truth, of raw feelings buried deep. We continued to meet and as time went by, this complete attentiveness for each other incredibly increased. We created a passport that opened up the love country to us. To tell of unique feelings we had.

However this ideal relationship was not, nor ever could be perfect: she had a husband. In the early days this wasn't a problem we quite simply enjoyed this magical friendship, but I suppose it was inevitable - the casual touch of hands became a clasp, the brief goodbye hold became an embrace, then finally the perfunctory peck on the cheek became an ardent kiss.

"What are we doing? Where are we going Brian?" She pleaded

"We haven't done anything wrong," I replied, knowing that it wasn't an answer and knowing that she knew it wasn't.

"He's such a good man you see." Desperation poured from her.

"Yes," I said inanely. "Yes, I know."

"Oh Brian-" The desperation deepening.

"We can't help our feelings Sheila." I'm searching for a way to go.

"No we can't, but there's a choice what we do about them." I didn't like the finality in her voice.

"I'll do anything you want Sheila, anything if we can be together."

"We can't make our happiness by destroying someone else's."

"What are you saying Sheila?"

I suppose it's goodbye darling."

It was to be a surgical parting: promises were made that neither of us would try to contact the other and the promises were kept.

It was about four weeks later. I'd taken a weekend break at a country pub in an attempt at a distraction from the emptiness I felt. It brought back morose memories of long years ago when my wife had died.

I was having lunch. I sensed rather than saw them. I looked up. They were walking towards me.

"Brian." There was a forced smile on her. "Fancy meeting you here." She had a gaunt, haggard look about her.

"Well..." Is all I could get out.

"Hello Brian," he said. "Small world."

"Yes, yes" I stammered. "But-but will you join me?"

In the circumstances, the lunch was bearable, if not pleasant, another bottle of wine and a brandy eased the tension.

However, I couldn't believe what I heard next. He asked me if I would take care of Sheila. He had to attend an interview and had intended taking Sheila with him, but she hadn't been well as perhaps I could see and it would be much better for her to enjoy the country instead of her hanging around all day waiting for him. After all the pleasantries it was arranged.

We made exquisite love.

She saw it when looking into her travel bag on leaving the room. A white envelope. As she read the letter I saw her face change, profuse tears slid unheeded down her cheek. He wrote that he knew of our liaison and that it grieved him, not only for his own hurt but also because he could see how her faithfulness to him was costing the suffering written on her face and this created a more grievous hurt in him and so after long torturous thoughts, he made the decision to let her go. He wrote that he loved her deeply and always would; if she ever needed him for whatever reason he would be there for her. He went on to say that he realized that neither Brian nor she had looked for this affair and felt sure I would take good care of her. He told her he loved her again and said he was going to take up a promotional post in Europe. I knew what this letter would mean.

Sheila kissed me goodbye and returned to her husband.

Deep within the heart, far from the ego, lies a sublime pure, unselfish creative spirit. The celestial fire of created love.

Adrian Spendlow (York)

Brynhildr – Mistreated Queen
(*brin-hild*)

Brynhildr is a mystical chooser of the dead, a swan, a raven, a beautiful woman, a waitress, a queen of warrior women, a Frayja rival, a flying woman, a mind controller, a burning corpse, a horse rider, a loving bride, a naked swimmer, broken hearted, tricked, toenail collector, a lovelorn fiancé, a hero worshipper, a battle
watcher, a trapped soul, a flying-ship builder, a cursed Valkyr, an assassin, a resurrected leader, Valhalla filler, Ragnarok recruiter, Brynhildr is beautiful, beautiful, beautiful, beautiful...

Armoured, shapely, mystical warrior Queen who chooses the valiant to die: shape changer she often would tire of her duties and swan-form swoop down to earth to un-feather and lady-naked swim in crisp clear waters. Some man stole her feather-skin and trapping her demanded that she used her powers over men to change the way of war. The loser, being a favourite of Odin's, caused rage and revenge and brought the curse of human mortality. Valkyr no longer she, trapped, would slumber forever in a mighty castle within a ring of fire. A hero was her only chance of happiness: Saved by brave Sigurdr, they fell in love and vowed to wed.

She was betrayed when poor cursed Sigurdr was given a love potion by Queen Grunhild to love her princess daughter Gudrun. All to gain Sigurdr's gold!

Shape-changing trickery and more leaping through flames forced heart-broken numb Brynhildr to agree to wed Gudrun's brother, Gunnar. Broken Brynhildr arranged Sigurdr's murder then cutting through her own heart fell wailing into his burning funeral pyre.

When worlds end and Valkyr call all to war it is hoped that her heart can rise to the task of leading the great and the good and the friends of gods.

Brynhildr is a mystical chooser of the dead, a swan, a raven, a beautiful woman, a waitress, a queen of warrior women, a Frayja rival, a flying woman, a mind controller, a burning corpse, a horse rider, a loving bride, a naked swimmer, broken hearted, tricked, toenail collector, a lovelorn fiancé, a hero worshipper, a battle
watcher, a trapped soul, a flying-ship builder, a cursed Valkyr, an assassin, a resurrected leader, Valhalla filler, Ragnarok recruiter,

Brynhildr is beautiful, beautiful, beautiful, beautiful...

Adrian Spendlow (York)

Died I Did

I died, in the hands of Helen
Because of her I became dead again
She brought me back, hurtling back
Then killed me again with a cushion
Crushed I was, to discover
What had happen in my past life
Regressive in effect
At the murderous hands of this dynamo
Crushed, crushed by a cushion
'Did the huge stone block',
As she prepared to dramatically drop,
'Feel like this?'
Yes, it did (my eyes were closed)
My eyes were closed forever
Moving me away from this life
Well, that life
She led me away from the light
Into another existence
Trapped there now still
In splendour remain, in the simple previous
I thank you Helen
Yours entirely regressed, for I
Am a worm, a
Worm

(Adrian is Poet-in-Residence at the Jorvik Centre for
York Archeological Trust, and a full-time poet and story-teller)

John Stocks   (Sheffield)

In the Showroom Cinema

This is a place to fall in love
To share a joke, a glass of wine
The time of day, and later watch
As autumn twilight gathers in.

And this is the place to observe
The rain, the way you toss your hair
When you walk in,
The sensuous intelligence
In your subtle, ironic smile.

To watch you as you read your book
Occasionally looking up
To cast your eye on the stranger
Who is loitering at the bar.

This is the time to fall in love
With the first soft mist of autumn
Rising from the crush of autumn leaves
And a sharp chill in the northern air.

This is the place to fall in love
And chase oblivion with a kiss
That crackles like a Samhain fire
And intimates a journey to
The landscape of your future dreams
The creative madness of desire.

John Stocks   (Sheffield)

Summer

What is it we dream of
when the sun has waltzed the clouds
away and suddenly stilled the sky
to the azure serenity of childhood summers?

Do we dream of mothers
forever young in July dresses
the innocence of early play
the callow softness of our skin?

Or lovers as we doze
the afternoon away
the scents that still ignite desire
the brief fireworks of ecstasy?

Or the drift from eloquence to silence
the infinite contours
of nostalgia
a subtle murmur of some distant now?

Or do we dream of the souls we have lost
the heavy resonance
of those we have loved
when passing clouds
obscure the sun?

Their fears, their hopes, their hopelessness
the thousand dreams we shared
before we were born.

Paul Sutherland   (Market Rasen)

Peter's Visit to His First Wife

At work, as Peter began cleaning and hoovering an advertising agency, his first wife phoned. Her distress shot through him. After the last employees left, Peter broke down on the stairs' uncarpeted landing. Unable to do his normal tasks, he walked across to the White Swan, after setting the alarm and locking up; but leaving the lights on. In the lit-up pub, some workers, Friday-tired and-relieved, some whom Peter knew, waved him over to join them. With his Canada Dry the middle-aged cleaner sat down with young ambitious work-dressed souls from another agency.

He noticed, overhead, china plates and serving bowls in a series tilting on round edges along a precarious wooden shelf: colourfully printed with ideals - stability, longevity - among them a willow pattern. He sometime collected willow patterns, but not pieces like those in a row above too rare and expensive, far beyond his range.

Peter resolved to go and see his ex-wife. He closed up the agency, turning off each light in correct succession and carefully punching in the alarm code. He strolled past glamorous evening couples up-town, hand in hand or hand in hers or his back jean pocket, until he reached a terrace-canyon with dim lighting and few passers-by. Hers wasn't an uncivil street (no rubbish bins dumped and screaming children) but everyone seemed afraid and stayed indoors all the time behind drawn curtains. For a minute, Peter was proud he lived in a rangy communal house with its confusion, disrespectful lodgers and over-stretched kitch-en; with its difficult won privacies and loud-music youths, but with its arm-chair living room and its lawns and trees, now in pale autumn colours.

His ex was in bed, downstairs in the small front room. When he lived here it had been his study. Despite the tone of her phone call, she was surprised to see him. Face to face, they talked kindly, even generously, over a plate of fish and chips; she took a few nibbles, emptying out the fish's white meat for herself then passing on the crisp batter to a grateful but cautious Peter. Her room appeared comfortable, if minute; easily exhausted by its mantelpiece congested with cards, books and soft toys. More creatures gathered at the foot of her bed in a heaped convention; a white and brown furry blur with black or other colour glass eyes that stared speechlessly at this intruder. He couldn't forget how professional she used to be with her cigarettes, straight skirts, training meetings and I-want-the-world postures which had strangely attracted him. So totally uncluttered.

Before he left, they embraced. Of course, Peter understood she was ill. He had often imagined that somehow she was doomed. So why had he married her? Now he could only hope the pain would desert his once love and a new life begin. 'You always make me feel at peace when you put your arms round me,' she now whispered. Their embrace lingered longer than Peter expected. If only I could make you feel peaceful from a distance with imaginary hugs, he dreamed. He felt her cheek skin press, gently pimpled and easily alarmed, upon his coarser cheek.

The act of leaving, they'd recognised, had always been hard, whether for a long or short duration. A slight parting could end in a row followed by a door-slamming departure. Perhaps they desired to be locked in each other's arms; each resenting who broke off first. Peter figured this situation meant insecurity, brittle as fine china. His first wife considered the consequence of their over-experienced lives; meant too much honesty, too many confrontations and naturally perpetual distrust.

This time, after a faint, controlled tug-of-war of 'I'm going/I'm not...', he broke free and slipped out the worn front door without a quarrel. Instead of going back to his, at this hour, ruckus home, he climbed an out-of-town hill and gazed up to observe the mid-October night spanned with glinting constellations. Bed-ridden, his estranged wife would soon be under going a dangerous operation.

But it wouldn't be his task, he reflected, to sit patiently by her semi-conscious body laid out on a hospital bed.

(Paul Sutherland is a well-published freelance poet/writer and editor of the distinguished literary arts journal Dream Catcher. He runs a variety of creative writing activities, working with a large range of abilities, ages and ethnicities in such places as community centres, libraries, schools and in higher education, art centres, museums with writing groups or with individual writers on a one to one basis)

Jemma Sykes   (Rotherham)

Dun't Be Bitter

"E's not gunna be best pleased when 'e get's in 'ere." said Ken, 'as e' fiddled wi' 'is 'earin' aid.

"There's nowt I can do abart it." John said from be'ind 'bar as 'e tried 'Tetley's pump for 'fifteenth time. "They're not having it."
There wa' 'alf empty glasses o' bitter all o'er bar.

'Clock be'ind bar ticked to half nine and all o' regulars looked ovva at dooer. They could 'ear his feet comin' darn steps artside. You could 'ave set your clock by Big Baz. 'Is routine ant changed in thirty years, along wi' 'is dress sense. 'E 'obbled up t' bar and took art 'is comb. 'E brushed 'sides o' 'is grey 'air back and put 'is comb back in 'is pocket like 'e alus did even though 'ten second walk from 'is 'ouse to 'pub dint mess it up. 'E rested 'is arms on bar and said "pint o' Tetleys please cocker."

"Soz Baz mate, all bitter's off." John said, grateful that 'e weren't in punchin' distance.

Baz looked 'round at 'other regulars and saw all their glasses wa' empty an' all. "Tha what?." Baz said so loud Ken 'ad to fiddle wi' 'is 'earin' aid aggen.

"Nowt a can do Baz"

"Reight." Baz said as 'e started walkin' towards 'dooer.

"Weear y gooin?" Ken sharted after 'im.

"'Someweear else." Baz sharted back.

'Regulars looked at each other. This wa' un'eard of. They all got up and follad 'im art o' dooer.

By 'time Baz got t' top o' steps, he wa' shattered. 'E'd just walked darn the ruddy things. 'E looked darn street, it wa' abart another ten minutes walk to next pub and it wa' one of them trendy pubs an' all. All loud music and young kids sharting at top o' the' voices. 'Nearest shop that sold bitter wa' at bottom o' 'ill and there weren't no way 'e wa' walkin' back up that wi' some cans.

Baz turned 'round to see all o' others pantin' their way up 'steps.

"There's somet not reight 'appening 'ere." 'e said as they got t' 'top. "Why 'as all bitter run 'art today? It wa' fine yesterday and y' can't run art of it all at once. What 'ave all your lot bin drinkin'?"

"We wa' on that reduced ale, 'e's sellin' it at a quid a pint at 'minute. 'Tastes like cat's piddle." said Ken.

"E' wa' tryin' to flog me that last week. 'E said it wa' gooin off." said Baz. "I reckon e's turned all o' bitter pumps off so 'e can get rid

86

o' that. We need to get in that cellar wi'art 'im seein' and get them pumps back on."

"Ere'yar John, some kids 'ave knocked ovva all o' benches artside." Baz said, lookin' red faced, sweatin' and art o' breath when 'e walked back into pub ten minutes layta.

"Mek shooer nobdi tampers wi' tills mate." John said as 'e walked towards dooer. Baz 'ad bin gooin in theear for years an' John knew 'e could trust 'im.

This wa' their chance. Ken, who wa' youngest o' lot at sixty three, shuffled be'ind bar and darn cellar steps. 'E knew 'e 'ad to be quick. E'd bin darn this pub cellar befooer but it wa' many moons ago. This pub wa' kind o' place wheear ev'ryone mucked in. If landlord needed an 'and doin' somet, you'd 'elp 'im art and get some free beer for your troubles. But y' still 'ad to watch 'em like hawks. They wa' crafty beggars when they wanted t' be.

Ken farnd the Tetleys keg and started t' turn 'tap on 'wire leading off o' it. It turned and 'e 'eard a glug comin' from 'barrel. 'E moved on t' John Smiths, then t' Stones and finally t' Worthin'tons. Movin' as fast 'as e' could, which weren't reight fast, 'e went back art in t' bar. E' just sat darn as John walked back in.

"Na then" Baz said as John walked back t' pumps. "pint o' Tetleys please cocker."

"Baz. A've said they're not workin'."

"Just try it so I can see it wi' mi own eyes." 'e replied.

"Alreight, but if owt comes art o' here, I'll gi y'all a free pint." 'e said looking 'round at 'four people in 'pub.

John pulled on 'pump and Tetleys started to fill 'pint pot below it. 'E looked shocked.

"Free pints all round then lads." Baz said as 'e 'eld up 'pint that John 'ad just gid him.

John moaned as 'e got a glass from below 'pumps t' start pourin' 'next un.

"Aw, come on John," laughed Baz, "dun't be bitter."

Adrian Tellwright   (York)

Nearly November

Time to try the central heating,
the week roof leaks reappear
and the clocks go back,
not that you can lie in bed that extra hour
with the slow regular pat pat overhead.

Nearly November
the coat tossed cyclist
wavers like an off green russet leaf.
The wind teeters between mild and chilly.
A small boy lifts a stick
waves it this way, that way -
will he, won't he -
urged on, urging a small scruff ball's
incessant bark bark barking.

Nearly November
starting to turn the edges,
crisp kickable up and over stout shoes,
dank apples and mushy conker shells,
smoke from a bonfire unfurls.
The cyclist's scarf loosens,
the smoke lingers,
then away from the dull glow
and intermittent snap crackle
worming diffusing,
slow pedal slow,
breathing in and out again.

Adrian Tellwright   (York)

Post-op Jotting

 The nurse is firm, friendly and direct.
'It's lights out.'

'But I like reading,
I like to see.
I like to write too,
to see to write.'

'D'you want any more painkillers?'

'"Remember to take a pad and pencil."
That's what a friend, a poet, said to me.
She's right. It helps to quell the pain.'

'Never mind that. Have you got enough pillows?'

'I'm a poet too. Well, I have been.
Is this where I get to rage
against the dying of the light?'

'Pull that cord if you need us.
I'm turning the light off.'

'Let me get to the end of the sentence.
There. You can go ahead now.'

Thank you, I will.'

'Good night.'

'Good night.'

Blessed are you, who heals all flesh
and performs such wonders.

Christine May Turner   (Rotherham)

Nights in White Cotton

Shadows dance on anaglypted wall,
expiring embers flicker a wordless tuneless lullaby,
Steadily, almost imperceivably eyelids fall,
the tut-tut of mantel clock faithful witness to contented sigh,
Charred wings of sooty composition flutter behind burning coals,
blue-grey wisps of smoke like tiny ascending souls
of long-slumbering fairy folk newly arisen,
What imaginings transpired in tired childhood eyes,
rebelling against a whispered, "Time for bed."
Shadow puppets on ceiling and sparks rising like fire-flies,
closed eyelids at last admit defeat leaving tears unshed,
Cocooned in warm flannelette, laid upon cool white cotton
to dream of tomorrows and hazy summer afternoons,
Dreaming dreams never to be forgotten, of daisy days,
life's ups and downs, and mystic madonna moons.

Christine May Turner   (Rotherham)

Dilemma

What is age but a measure of days,
How do I love thee, let me count the ways.
What is age but a measure began at birth,
A measure of time to be spent on earth.
What is age but a well-worn face,
Youth, when lost, we cannot replace.
What is age when time's flown too fast,
Wanting and needing the pleasure to last.
What is age but a journey we've made,
Relived in our mind lest the memory should fade.
What is age should you come to love another,
Don't judge a book (don't they say) by its cover.
What is age if not a state of mind,
Would we judge every face if our eyes were blind.
What is age if not a mirror of the soul,
With love you can go on, feel cherished, feel whole.
What is age, must it be the decider,
Whether to let go of love or open arms wider?

Clint Wastling   (York)

The Fixture

It was a crunch match for city and a crunch time for Clarissa. She'd scrimped and saved for her son's birthday treat and even did an extra shift at the club, thanks to her mother babysitting, so it was a great feeling watching the premiership teams limber up.

Clarissa sat with her fingers warming round a cup of coffee. Daniel looked half as big again wearing a hand-me-down fleece and hat but he refused to wear gloves, "Mum, I need to tick off the teams as they're announced!" And so he sat with his pen at the ready and his PSP stowed in his pocket for once.

Money was tight and any extra went on making sure Daniel got the things he should and paying off that loan. It had been a stupid moment of weakness, two hundred quid had multiplied quickly to four hundred. Clarissa knotted her handkerchief round her fingers. Daniel put his small hand over hers.

"You're my number one!" she said with pride.

"And City are mine!" he replied missing the point. Daniel knew every match statistic and as the game got underway, he provided a commentary. "See Altidore, he was great last week on the front line, he's been partnered with Fagan, still... it's a crunch game."

There's only one city. The crowd roared. The red and whites had made a good start and Etherington threatened on the break and with a deft kick, curled the ball into the net. It was only twenty nine minutes in. Daniel sighed. Everyone fell silent. It was as if the final whistle had already blown.

"Get at em!" the old man behind shouted as they took the centre. The cry was picked up and soon the chanting began again. The punter along from them said, "He'll have to go!" The man pointed at the manager.

"There's still the second half!" Danny said in reply. Phil could do no wrong in his eyes; after all he got them in the top flight. They climbed the steps and entered the corridor accompanied by the smells of hot dogs and with warm coffee. "I think they'll be a new team in the second half, he's got a classic four-four-two and that suits them."

Clarissa nodded as they queued for drinks and crisps. "Quick!" Clarissa pulled Danny into a recess as a tall thin man with a large gold bracelet and chain walked by. "Someone I don't want to meet!" She said pointedly. The man peered around the room. He was looking for someone. Clarissa remained hidden until the man was engulfed by the crowd.

I owe him money." she admitted to Daniel, "that's something you must promise - neither a lender nor a borrower be, as my old dad used to say. If only I'd listened."

City came out fighting in the second half and Jimmy Bullard was the catalyst for some great ball play. Daniel got his scarf and closed his eyes, praying for a goal. He didn't have to wait long. Olofinjana scored and the crowd erupted. Bullard harried and created lots of opportunities. Clarissa sensed the mood lift; suddenly it felt as though City could win. There was some sort of ruckus near the line and the ref took out a yellow card and followed it with a red. Daniel stood on the step to see. It was a red and white player and the opposition were down to ten men. City quickly took advantage and drew blood in the ninetieth when Hesselink scored. The elation and relief turned the air electric as the crowd chanted "Two-one, two-one." And people jabbed the air with their fingers. Danny sang until his voice croaked. The whistle blew. City were out of the relegation zone.

"Can we stay and get autographs?" Danny asked.

"Ok, but some warm soup first before we stand and wait, my feet are freezing!"

"I know where to wait, I read it on the internet."

Clarissa ruffled his hair and smiled. When they got outside the ground, the crowds had leaked away and there were just a few posh cars left, black BMWs and top of the range Range Rovers with darkened windows.

Danny waited by the changing room exit, pen and programme poised.

"Hello Clarissa." The gaunt young man appeared from nowhere. His gold chain sparkled in the sun. "You're behind with the instalments."

Daniel moved closer to his mum, sensing the danger. The man smiled, "lovely family scene, shame to spoil it." He held out his hand expecting a gift.

Clarissa pushed her son behind her and moved forward. "The trouble with people like you is that you rely on victims. Well I'm not going to be a victim anymore."

The man smiled and produced a cosh.

Clarissa took out her mobile and started videoing. "Go on then." The loan shark looked around. There were several players emerging from the changing rooms. He lost his nerve.

"Go get those autographs!"

Daniel hesitated.

"Go on, I'll be fine. When I've finished this conversation, it's the police and an appointment at citizen's advice. I'm getting you sorted!"

The man seemed to diminish. He stared at her, "I want my money back."

"Oh!" Clarissa replied, "You'll get everything you're due." She smiled and walked over, Danny's match programme was rapidly filling with signatures and he was chatting with his heroes like a long lost friend.

A. K. Whitehead   (Pontefract)

The Companion

We grew old together,
never meeting.
Me with neither fame
nor fortune,
he with a bank-full of both.
But he had talent and ability
that carried him without distain
when most others failed
to make the cutting room again.

I watched him change from role to role,
bending and weaving, moving
through complexities of time
and eventually betrayal of skin and flesh,
the sagging parts when now undressed,
where muscle had embraced a traitor's role
when once it had invested every part.

I knew him well through all those years
and shared a hundred square feet of air
when once he opened up a store.
He kept his hair when mine had gone

though I kept my wife when he had lost all four
and I was sorry for him there...

he not having known such wealth
as I still had to share.

A. K. Whitehead   (Pontefract)

Falling Cages

We cursed the cages that came up and fell here
and buried men and beasts, greatest and least
alive in the dark hewn caverns of lightless
night, cheated of air that the wheatchaff
and blackbird knew, nor lacking the water
that saw no earth nor foe but travelling
as far to the black seams where foreign stars
could not encase themselves. "No place," we said
"for even the dead," though now and then dread
sirens could mark tombs of blood and broken
bones, signified by blackness known only
underground.

And we have found this levelled
site where now the linnets sing a rare song
and shades of men, watched yet by shadows
of their women, still tramp wearing pack and lamp
and disappear where no gear drops a cage.

Clouds

Clouds want privacy where they see
most beauty, boasting of their finds,
for clouds are changed by what they enshroud
and seek to cling to things and, like
a woman's ointments, hide the joins
and trick the years with their thin veneers.

Clouds cling to England to preserve
what will attract them most in their pact
with nature. There are higher moors
and hills elsewhere that thrill the clouds
far less, for their preference is
for a pinnacle with no twin:
the highest form that verifies
and will attest the greatest skill.

Sue Whittaker   (York)

An Old Complaint

His breath does not come
so easily nowadays.
Silica dust fibrosis
clusters in his lungs.
A heavy weight on chest.
Sleep does not come
as a peaceful support.
Nights are long.
Light a welcome.
His vacation is permanent.
Seaside air a treat.
Sanitorium rest.
Cure antibiotically slow.

Sue Whittaker   (York)

Birdwatch

I tightly wrap my wings to keep me from
the wind and view winter from rickety fence.
Squint through blizzard-covered A66
while traffic seeks a safer place.
Motor panorama white, layer upon layer.
No-man's-land freezes and brave ones plough.
Wind and more snow drops to a steady breeze.
Our cackle just heard over trapped users.
They amuse us. In winter months no-one wins.
Except us. On the make.
Black iridescent smooth jacks.
Sit waiting to scavenge like spivs.

Bernadette Whiteley   (Barnsley)

Sonnet For a New Baby

Can I bear to share him yet with the world?
In the quiet afterwards, peacefully,
we marvel at his perfect symmetry.
You and I in miniature, fingers curled
fast round my own. His future unfurls
beyond this moment. We spin our dreams while
Time drifts on, beyond the room.
One minute more, till we let in the world.

Gently, we touch the pulse of his quick heart,
Quivering beneath his black velvety hair,
Feel his quick breath brushing against our skin.
The world rushes in, the silence departs.
Cocooned in the soft cradle of our care,
Are you ready, child, for life to begin?

Bernadette Whiteley   (Barnsley)

The Glass Factory   (30693)

The silence startled him at first,
like suddenly slipping underwater
and finding nothing to cling to.
Words were jewels, seldom shared.
Ear plugs muffled the constant clamour of mechanical arms
picking and placing,
picking and placing,
picking and placing.
Their hypnotic robotic dance
entranced his homesick soul.
Soon the silence is a comfort,
a curtain to hide behind.
Alone amongst an army of machines,
he bathes in his native language,
swims in the songs,
paddles in poems and prayers,
and drifts through rose-tinted memories,
while the factory's silent movie plays on.

Louise Wilford (Elsecar)

Clee Hills

The wind nags, up here, above the cloud-line. Fog's
wet feathers on your skin, an eiderdown dipped in the sea,
- as if the world ends at your fingertips. You guide yourself
by fence-posts, feeling out the livestock like a game
of Blind Man's Buff. You're eyeless at the edges.
But still, the wind's worse, the piercing groan of it.

The land up here's scooped out, piled up, abandoned.
Generations of poor sods worked eight-hour
shifts, after an hour's uphill tramp, hacking at the dhustone
with 28lb hammers. Sometimes they slept here, days lined up
like dominoes. Old mine shafts capped with brick domes
are bubbles in the hillside that could pop at a wrong step.

The landscape slips and slithers. Stumps of pylon footings
like old men's teeth, spoil heaps like dragon's dugs,
the flimsy needle of a radio-mast poised to scratch the sky.
Great-granddad was a face-man on the Clee.
He taught my mum, aged two, to ride a horse, stirrups
dangling, straps rolled up so she could get her feet in.

Pools of black tar left over from the workings catch
the sheep like birdlime. Even now I still find wind-dried
 sheep bones on the flanks and in the crevices. The rain
paints the sky grey as pewter. No one leaves the Hills.
There's generations here, each knowing every other.
Fog sticks us to these slopes. Seeps into our skin.

Sometimes, you look down at the clouds below,
a white-grey ocean of mist caught in a still-shot
as if time has stopped. You hear only the wind's eerie
whistle. A sheep's bleat. Your heartbeat. You could drift over
that sea, canvas sails wind-filled. You could climb the hill's
rigging to the crow's nest and watch the white-grey waves.

Louise Wilford (Elsecar)

Firing Squad

Strange how it comes to this, the distant black astonished mouths
settling into a steady row, ready to spit

> Elizabeth standing by the upright piano
> cock-eyed red cross

The grass is trampled here. Mud leaks through fronds of weed,
the dance-floor for a score of twitching men. St Vitas. Crispin Crispianus

> the high pink smell of moor-top heather
> giant blades of granite
> siren hoot

in a split slice of a second, I glimpse a kestrel, black scratch in the
half-cooked sky, breathing a tower of air, dropping

> And then Elizabeth.
> blond eye-lash on her ashen cheek

strange how I'll never touch

Who will tell her? A blank white hand with a telegram
afraid to say I shook like a marionette   my bowels burned
they'll have to scrub the stench off the khaki later
when they cart off what's left   tongue pressing palette   teeth
chattering   arms jerking as the clicks   like children's
claps   like nails on teeth   dog's claws on pavements   belt buckles
harness rings

> the kestrel drops
> in a cloudless yellow dawn

*(The original version of 'Clee Hills' won the Mike Haywood Competition
a few years ago (think it was 2006) and was later published in 'Agenda'.
This is a more updated (and 1 think better) version:)*

101